WAR DEPARTMENT

BASIC FIELD MANUAL

U. S. CARBINE, CALIBER .30, M1

May 20, 1942

parkerpub.co

Published by Parker Publishing Company

www.parkerpub.co

BASIC FIELD MANUAL

*

U. S. CARBINE, CALIBER .30, M1

UNITED STATES

GOVERNMENT PRINTING OFFICE

WASHINGTON : 1942

WAR DEPARTMENT,

WASHINGTON, May 20, 1942.

FM 23-7, U. S. Carbine, Caliber .30, M1, is published for the information and guidance of all concerned.

[A. G. 062.11 (4-24-42).]

BY ORDER OF THE SECRETARY OF WAR:

G. C. MARSHALL,

Chief of Staff.

OFFICIAL:

J. A. ULIO,

Major General,

The Adjutant General.

DISTRIBUTION:

R 1-7, 10, 11, 17, 18 (3); Bn 2-7, 9-11, 17-19 (3); IBn 1 (3); C 2, 5-7, 17, 18 (20); 3, 4, 9, 10, 19 (10); IC 1, 11 (20).

(For explanation of symbols see FM 21-6.)

TABLE OF CONTENTS

SCORE CARD FOR CARBINE M-1

(Name)

(ASN)   (Organization)

Targets_____	Standing and sitting	100 yards				Total
Order_____						
Date_____						

(Signature of scorer)   (Signature of officer)

Targets_____	Standing and kneeling	100 yards				Total
Order_____						
Date_____						

(Signature of scorer)   (Signature of officer)

Targets_____	Standing and sitting	200 yards				Total
Order_____						
Date_____						

(Signature of scorer)   (Signature of officer)

Targets_____	Standing and kneeling	200 yards				Total
Order_____						
Date_____						

(Signature of scorer)   (Signature of officer)

Targets_____	Standing to prone	300 yards				Total
Order_____						
Date_____						

(Signature of scorer)   (Signature of officer)

Qualification: Grand aggregate_____

Date_____, 19__   Certified correct:

Commanding Co_____

IV

BASIC FIELD MANUAL

U. S. CARBINE, CALIBER .30 M1

CHAPTER I

MECHANICAL TRAINING

SECTION I

GENERAL

■ 1. DESCRIPTION OF CARBINE.—The U. S. carbine, caliber .30, M1, is a self-loading shoulder weapon (see fig. 1). It is gas operated, magazine fed, and air cooled. It weighs approximately 5 pounds. The weapon is fed from a box type magazine having a capacity of 15 rounds.

■ 2. GENERAL DATA.—*a. Dimensions.*—(1) *Barrel.*
Diameter of bore_____inches__ .30
Number of grooves_____   4
Length of barrel_____inches__ 17.75
(2) *Carbine.*
Over-all length of carbine_____inches__ 35.50
Sight radius_____do____ 22.
b. Weight.
Carbine without sling_____pounds__ 5.12
Carbine with sling_____do____ 5.23
Magazine, empty_____do____   .17
Magazine, loaded_____do____   .57
Total weight w/sling and loaded
magazine_____do____ 5.80

1

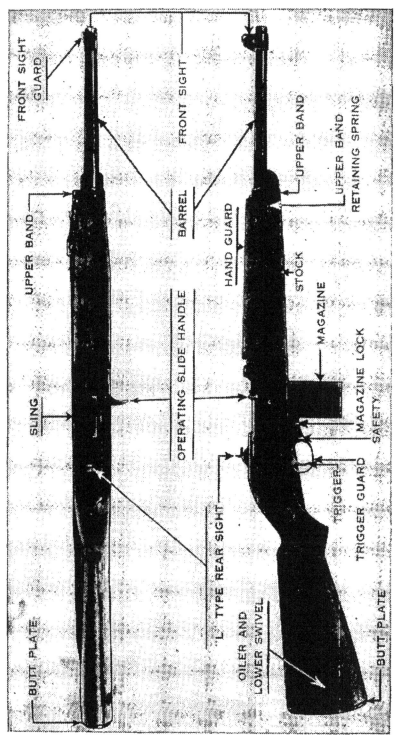

FIGURE 1.—U. S. carbine, caliber .30, M1.

■ 3. MISCELLANEOUS DATA.

    Muzzle velocity_____feet per second__ 1900
    Pressure in chamber (approx.)
           pounds per square inch__ 40,000
    Weight of ball cartridge (approx.)
                   grains__   195
    Weight of bullet (approx.) _____grains__   110

■ 4. REAR SIGHT.—*a*. Models of the carbine initially issued will be equipped with an L-type rear sight, consisting of

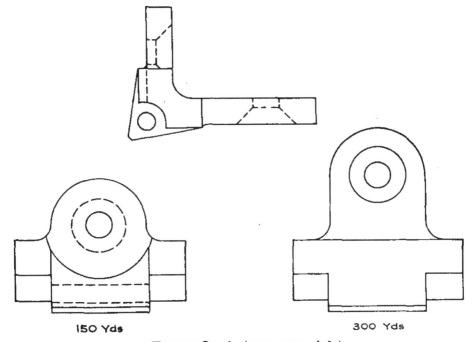

    150 Yds   300 Yds

FIGURE 2.—L-type rear sight.

two arms at right angles, each pierced with an aperture. A flat spring is placed between the sight leaf and sight base to retain the sight leaf in position. Either sight may be raised into position by turning with the fingers, and the leaf is held correctly by the pressure of the spring. The apertures provided are computed for ranges of 150 and 300 yards. With this sight it will be necessary to aim off the target to secure intermediate changes in range and windage corrections. (See fig. 2.)

3

b. Later models of the carbine will be equipped with an adjustable sight generally similar to that shown in other figures in this manual. This sight will be graduated from 100 to 300 yards in increments of 50 yards and will provide for 3 points of left and 3 points of right windage. The amount which changes of elevation and windage will move the point of strike must be determined by experiment.

■ 5. FRONT SIGHT.—The front sight is the post type, protected by wings and adjusted laterally during assembly at the arsenal. It is locked in position, after adjustment, by riveting part of the metal base into the lock seat with a punch.

■ 6. NOMENCLATURE AND REFERENCES.—*a. Nomenclature.*—The soldier should be familiar with the names of those parts of the carbine which are frequently referred to in drill and range practice (figs. 3 to 6, inclusive).

b. References.—Safety precautions to be observed by troops are complete in this manual. Range officers, the officer in charge of firing, and the commander responsible for the location of ranges and conduct of firing should refer to AR 750–10 for additional safety precautions.

SECTION II

DISASSEMBLY AND ASSEMBLY

■ 7. WHEN TAKEN UP.—Training in disassembly and assembly is taken up as soon as practicable after the soldier receives his carbine. This training is completed before the individual does any firing with the weapon.

■ 8. ORGANIZATION.—In the company or platoon, men armed with the carbine are organized into one or more groups under their officers or selected noncommissioned officers as instructors and supervisors.

■ 9. CARE TO BE EXERCISED.—*a.* The carbine can be readily disassembled and assembled without applying force. The application of force is prohibited.

b. The weapon will not be disassembled or assembled against time. In all practice in disassembling the carbine, individuals will be taught to lay the parts out on a smooth, clean surface in the proper sequence for assembling.

■ **10. DISASSEMBLING.**—*a. General.*—Disassembly of the carbine by the soldier is limited to those steps required for proper care and maintenance of the weapon. Further disassembly will not be made except under the supervision of an officer or ordnance personnel. Only the following parts may be removed by the individual soldier without supervision:

> Sling and oiler (and lower sling swivel).
> Magazine.
> Hand guard.
> Stock assembly.
> Operating slide spring.
> Operating slide spring guide rod.
> Guard assembling pin.
> Trigger group assembly.
> Operating slide.
> Bolt assembly.
> Barrel and receiver assembly.

b. Sequence.—The disassembly of the carbine authorized to be performed by the soldier without supervision is made in the following sequence:

(1) *Sling and oiler (and lower sling swivel).*—Unsnap and remove sling from the upper sling swivel. Remove oiler and attached sling from the recess in the butt of the stock.

(2) *Magazine.*—Hold the carbine, muzzle to the front, between the right side of the body and right forearm. Hold the magazine with the left hand. With the thumb of the right hand, press the magazine lock from the right side to the left and withdraw the magazine downward out of the receiver. *CAUTION: Do not let the magazine drop to the ground.*

(3) *Hand guard.*—Place the carbine on a level surface, resting the muzzle so that the head of the upper band screw is up and to the left. Using the rim of a carbine cartridge, loosen the upper band screw about ⅛ inch. Turn the barrel over. Depress the upper band retaining spring with the base of the cartridge, and slide the upper band over the retaining spring and off the stock. With the left hand, slide the hand guard forward until its rear end is disengaged from the groove in the front end of the receiver, and remove the hand guard from the barrel.

(4) *Stock assembly.*—Grasp the small of the stock with the right hand and the barrel with the left hand, palm up.   Push the safety to the left.   Raise the muzzle end of the barrel from the stock until the receiver is released from the stock abutment.   Remove the stock from the barrel, trigger group assembly, and receiver.

(5) *Operating slide spring and guide rod.*—Place the barrel and attached assemblies on a level surface, muzzle to

HAND GUARD

BARREL, RECEIVER, OPERATING SLIDE AND
TRIGGER GROUP ASSEMBLY

STOCK

FIGURE 3.—Three main groups, U. S. carbine, caliber .30, M1.

the left, operating slide handle up.   Grasp the operating spring guide rod between the thumb and forefinger of the right hand and pull the rod to the rear, disengaging it from its seat in the operating slide.   Raise the rod slightly and withdraw the operating spring to the left from its well in the receiver (see fig. 7).   Separate the spring from its guide rod.

(6) *Trigger group assembly.*—Cock the hammer by pulling the operating slide to the rear and pushing it forward.   Turn

the barrel so that the operating slide handle is down. Punch the guard assembling pin from its seat by starting it with the small end of the operating spring guide rod held in the right hand. Pull out pin from far side with left hand.

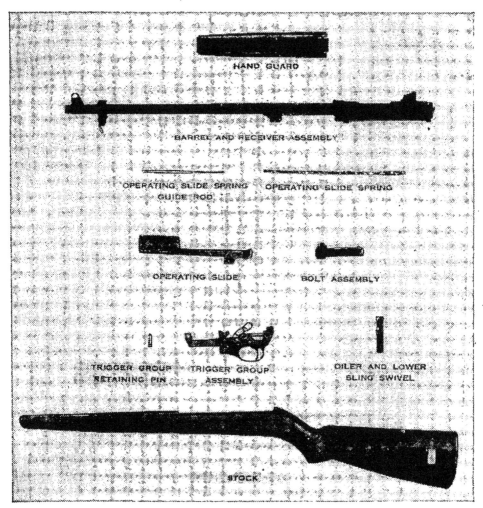

FIGURE 4.—Groups and parts to be removed for care and cleaning.

Grasp the barrel with the left hand and the trigger group assembly with the right hand as shown in figure 8. The trigger group assembly may now be removed by sliding it to the left and disengaging its undercut grooves from the corresponding grooves in the receiver·

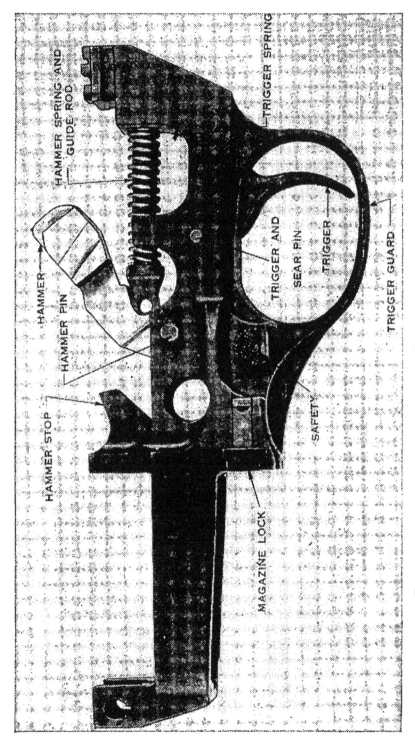

FIGURE 5.—Trigger group assembly with hammer in cocked position.

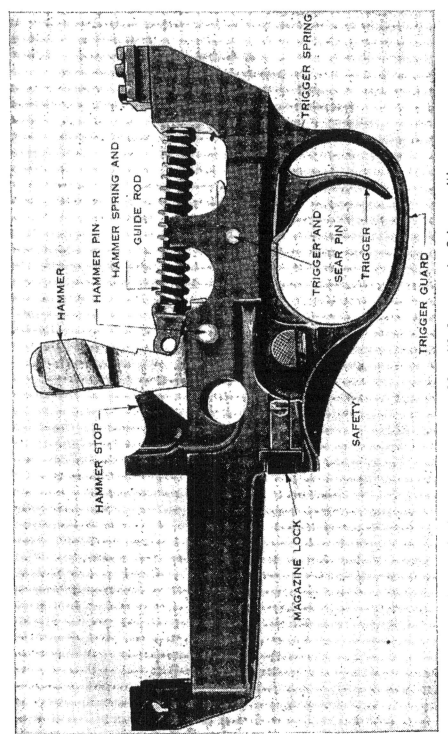

FIGURE 6.—Trigger group assembly with hammer in firing position.

(7) *Operating slide* (see fig. 9).—Rest the barrel on a level surface, muzzle to the front, receiver down. Hold the rear end of the receiver against the body with the left hand, thumb resting on top of the left side of the operating slide. Grasp the operating slide handle with the thumb and forefinger of the right hand and draw the slide slowly to the rear until the lug on the inner side of the rear end of the slide is opposite

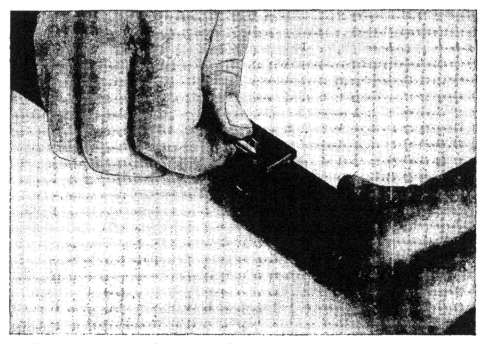

FIGURE 7.—Removing operating slide spring and guide rod.

the operating slide dismounting notch in the operating groove of the receiver. Pull the operating handle to the right and up and disengage the rear end of the slide from the operating lug on the bolt. The slide may now be removed from the barrel by a downward pressure of the left thumb on the left side of the slide, thus disengaging the lug on the slide from the left guiding groove in the under side of the barrel.

(8) *Bolt assembly.*—Hold the barrel as described in (7) above. Grasp the operating lug on the bolt between the thumb and forefinger of the right hand and move the bolt so that its front end is just in rear of the locking recesses in the receiver. Raise the front end of the bolt about 1 inch.

Rotate the bolt slightly to the right so that the tail of the firing pin is opposite its notch in the bottom of the receiver. Lift the bolt from the receiver.

■ 11. Assembling.—The carbine and its component groups are assembled in the reverse order of their disassembly.

    a. Bolt assembly.—Grasp the operating lug of the bolt

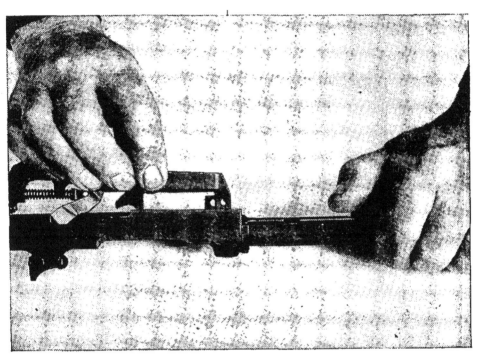

FIGURE 8.—Sliding trigger group assembly off receiver.

between the thumb and forefinger of the right hand. Hold the bolt so that the tail of the firing pin is opposite its notch in receiver, then lower the bolt into position.

    b. Operating slide.—Grasp the forward end of the slide in the right hand, palm up. Slide the bolt forward until its forward end is about 1½ inches from the chamber and hold it in this position with the left thumb. Engage the operating lug of the bolt in the operating cam groove of the slide. Raise the forward end of the slide so that the dismounting lug on its left side is opposite the notch in the left groove on the under side of the barrel. Then, by slightly twisting the slide to the right, engage the operating lugs of the slide in the operating grooves of the barrel. Move the slide and bolt to the rear until the operating slide lug is seated in its groove in the receiver. Close the bolt. (See fig. 10.)

c. Trigger group assembly.—Place the barrel and receiver on its left side, muzzle to the left. Replace the trigger group assembly by engaging its undercut grooves with the cor-

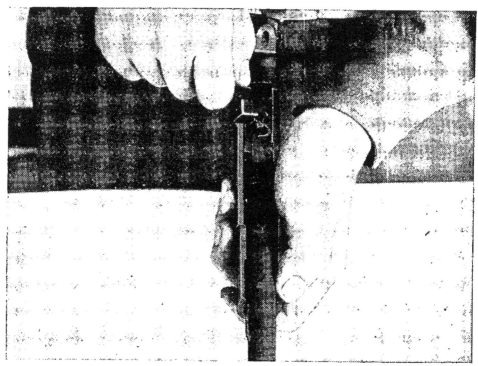

FIGURE 9.—Removing the operating slide.

responding grooves in the receiver. Replace the guard assembling pin.

d. Operating slide spring and guide rod.—Insert the small end of the guide rod in the loosely coiled end of the spring. Insert the closely coiled end of the spring into its well in the receiver. Steady the barrel with the left hand, and with the thumb and forefinger of the right hand on the shoulder of the guide rod, compress the spring so that the end of the guide rod may be inserted in its seat in the slide.

e. Stock assembly and hand guard.—Make certain the safety is to the left. Replace the barrel and assembled groups in the stock. Replace the hand guard. Slide the upper band down over the end of the hand guard and stock until it is engaged by the upper band retaining spring. Tighten the upper band screw.

f. Sling and oiler (and lower sling swivel).—Attach lower loop of the sling to the oiler. Replace the oiler in its recess in the stock. Attach upper end of the sling to the upper sling swivel.

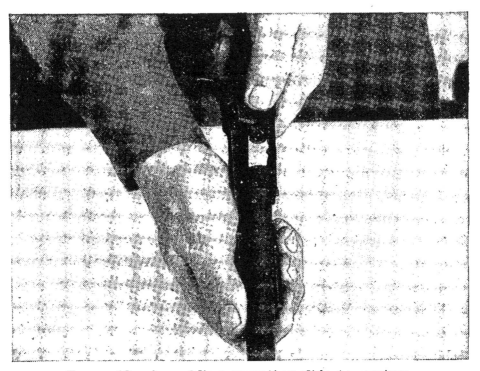

FIGURE 10.—Assembling operating slide to receiver.

SECTION III

CARE AND CLEANING

■ 12. GENERAL.—The attention given to a weapon of this type determines largely whether it will function properly and shoot accurately. The bore and chamber must be kept in good condition for accurate shooting. It is essential that the receiver and moving parts be kept clean, lubricated, and in good condition for reliability in functioning. Magazines must be kept free from rust, grit, gum, and dents or other damage in order to function properly.

■ 13. IN GARRISON AND CAMP.—*a. General.*—Keep the carbine well cleaned and oiled so as to preserve its condition and appearance during the periods when no firing is being done. Carbines in the hands of troops should be inspected daily to insure proper condition and cleanliness.

b. Bore.—The bore of the carbine will always be cleaned with a cleaning rod inserted from the muzzle. The rod used should be of such length as to permit cleaning the bore without damage to the face of the bolt. If a longer rod is used the bolt must be removed or the face of the bolt protected. This can be done in several ways. The simplest way is to cover the face of the bolt with a cloth stuffed into the receiver. To clean the bore, attach a cloth patch to the cleaning rod. Insert the cleaning rod into the bore at the muzzle and move it back and forth several times. Remove the patch. *CAUTION: In cleaning the bore, care must be taken not to foul the gas port with threads from the cleaning patch itself or with other extraneous matter.* Repeat until several successive patches come out absolutely clean. Inspect the bore. If the bore is clean, saturate a patch in light rust-preventive compound and swab the bore thoroughly so that all interior surfaces have a coating of the compound. If the bore still has residue in it swab it with a patch saturated with rifle bore cleaner, until it is clean, then apply the rust preventive.

c. Chamber.—The chamber should be cleaned when the bore is cleaned. A roughened or rusty chamber may cause cartridges to stick. To clean the chamber use a chamber cleaning brush and scrub the chamber vigorously. After this scrubbing, the chamber is further cleaned and oiled in the process of cleaning the bore.

d. Exterior surfaces.—To clean the screw heads and crevices, use a small cleaning brush or small stick. To clean the metal surfaces, wipe with a dry cloth to remove moisture, perspiration, and dirt; then wipe with a cloth containing a small quantity of light preservative lubricating oil. A light film of this oil should be applied to all moving parts, and this protective film should be maintained at all times. The stock and hand guard should be wiped with raw linseed oil.

e. Magazines.—It is imperative that magazines be given the best of care and kept in perfect condition. They should be disassembled, wiped clean and dry, and thinly coated with oil. Dirt that gets into them must be removed. In handling magazines, care should be taken to avoid denting or bending them, especially the lips of the mouth of the magazine.

f. After cleaning.—After cleaning the carbine, place it in the rack without covering and without a plug in the muzzle or chamber. Muzzle covers, carbine covers, rack covers, and plugs must not be used because they collect moisture and promote rust. To protect the carbines from dust, covers may be placed over racks when squad rooms or tents are swept; they must be removed after the rooms have been swept.

■ 14. PREPARATORY TO FIRING.—The following procedure before firing insures efficient functioning of the carbine:

a. Dismount main groups.

b. Wipe oil or grease from the bore.

c. Thoroughly clean and lightly oil all metal parts. Use light preservative lubricating oil.

d. Apply a thin, uniform coating of light preservative lubricating oil to the parts listed below:

(1) Bolt lugs (locking and operating).

(2) Bolt guides.

(3) Cocking cam on bolt.

(4) Piston.

(5) Contact surfaces of barrel and operating slide.

(6) Operating slide cam.

(7) Operating slide guide groove in receiver and barrel.

(8) Operating slide spring.

(9) Operating slide spring guide rod.

CAUTION: Do not apply oil to the under surface of the bolt, as the introduction of oil into the chamber may lead to the generation of excessive pressure.

e. Assemble carbine and rub all outer surfaces with a lightly oiled rag to remove dust.

■ 15. AFTER FIRING.—The bores of all carbines must be thoroughly cleaned by the evening of the day on which they are fired. They should be cleaned in the same manner for the next three days. *CAUTION: Under no circumstances will metal fouling solution be used in the carbine.*

a. Cleaning immediately after firing, or as soon as possible.—For this purpose water must be used; warm water is good, but warm, soapy water is better. Hold the carbine bottom side up, so that no water will enter the gas port. Run several wet patches through the bore. Remove the patch section from the cleaning rod, substitute the brush, and work this back and forth through the bore several times. Care should be used to see that the brush goes all the way through the bore before the direction is reversed. Detach the brush and run several wet patches through the bore, removing them from the breech end. Follow this with dry patches until the patches come out clean and dry. Saturate a patch in light preservative lubricating oil and push it through the bore, holding the rifle, top side up, so that some of the oil *will* flow into the gas port. *CAUTION: In cleaning the bore, be careful not to foul the cleaning patch in the gas port.*

b. Complete cleaning.—This cleaning should be done as soon as possible after that described in *a* above. If the carbine is to be fired the next day proceed as in paragraph 14. If the carbine is not to be fired in the next few days repeat procedure in *a* above for 3 days. In addition, the instructions prescribed in paragraphs 13 and 14 will be observed.

■ 16. ON RANGE OR IN FIELD.—The carbine must be kept clean and free from dirt and properly lubricated with oil. To obtain its maximum efficiency the following points must be observed:

a. Never fire a carbine with dust, dirt, mud, or snow in the bore.

b. Keep the chamber clean and free from oil and dirt.

c. Never leave a patch, plug, or other obstruction in the chamber or bore. Neglect of this precaution may result in serious injury.

d. If the carbine gives indications of lack of lubrication and excessive friction, apply additional oil to the parts. Excessive friction exists if the empty cases are being ejected to the right rear. When this occurs, oil should be applied at the first opportunity, as failures to feed and eject will occur if the condition is not corrected.

e. Keep a light coating of oil on all other metal parts.

f. Oil the piston without loosening the gas cylinder nut.

g. In general, it should not be necessary to remove any of the parts of the carbine in the field for cleaning except the trigger group assembly, the operating slide spring and rod, the operating slide and the bolt assembly.

h. During range firing a well-qualified man should be placed in charge of the cleaning of carbines at the cleaning racks or tables.

■ 17. PREPARATION FOR STORAGE.—*a.* Light preservative lubricating oil is the most suitable oil for preserving the mechanism of carbines. This oil is efficient for preserving the polished surfaces, the bore, and the chamber for a period of from 2 to 6 weeks, depending on the climatic and storage conditions.

b. Light rust-preventive compound is efficient for preserving the polished surfaces, the bore, and the chamber for a period of 1 year or less, depending on the climatic and storage conditions.

c. The carbine should be cleaned and prepared with particular care. The bore, all parts of the mechanism, and the exterior of the carbine should be thoroughly cleaned and then dried completely with rags. In damp climates particular care must be taken to see that the rags are dry. After drying a metal part it should not be touched with bare hands. All metal parts should then be coated either with light preservative lubricating oil or light rust-preventive compound, depending on the length of storage. (See *a* and *b* above.) Application of the rust-preventive compound to the bore of the carbine is best done by dipping the cleaning brush in the compound and running it through the bore two or three times. Before placing the carbine in the packing chest see that the bolt is in its forward position and that the firing pin is released. Paint the wooden supports at the butt and muzzle with rust-preventive compound. Then, handling the carbine by the stock and hand guard only, it should be placed in the packing chest. Under no circumstances should a carbine be placed in storage in a cloth or other cover or with a plug in the bore. Such articles collect moisture which causes the weapon to rust.

■ 18. CLEANING OF RIFLES AS RECEIVED FROM STORAGE.—*a.* Carbines which have been stored in accordance with paragraph 17 will be coated with either light preservative lubricating oil or light rust-preventive compound. Carbines received from ordnance storage will, in general, be coated with heavy rust-preventive compound. Use a dry-cleaning solvent to remove all traces of the compound or oil, particular care being taken that all recesses in which springs or plungers operate are cleaned thoroughly. After using the dry-cleaning solvent make sure it is completely removed from all parts. Then follow instructions contained in paragraph 13. If the carbines are to be fired immediately, follow instructions contained in paragraph 14.

b. Dry-cleaning solvent is a petroleum distillate used for removing grease. It is noncorrosive and of low inflammability. It is generally applied with rag swabs to large parts and as a bath for small parts. The surfaces must be thoroughly dried immediately after removal of the solvent. To avoid leaving finger marks, which are ordinarily acid and induce corrosion, gloves should be worn by persons handling parts after this cleaning. Dry-cleaning solvent will attack and discolor rubber.

SECTION IV

FUNCTIONING

■ 19. WHEN TAKEN UP.—Instruction in functioning will be taken up after instruction in the disassembly, assembly, and care and cleaning of the carbine.

■ 20. DESCRIPTION OF CYCLE.—*a. Rearward movement.*—(1) When the carbine is loaded and the bolt is closed, the hammer is held in the cocked position by the front end of the sear engaging in the sear notch on the hammer. The trigger lip under action of the trigger spring is seated under the rear end of the sear. If pressure is then applied to the trigger, the trigger pivots about the trigger pin causing the trigger lip to rise and carry with it the rear end of the sear. The sear also pivots about the trigger pin and now has its front end drawn downward to the point where it disengages from the sear notch on the hammer. The hammer, thus released, is actuated by the hammer spring which causes it to rotate about the hammer pin and strike the firing pin, through which its blow is transmitted to the primer of the cartridge. The above action can take place only if the tang of the firing pin is seated in the receiver. This cannot occur unless the bolt is fully rotated into its locked position. If the hammer should strike the firing pin when the bolt is in any other position the cartridge will not fire; the effect will be to deaden the hammer blow and rotate the bolt toward its locked position. In addition, the safety must be in its off position so that it will not lock the trigger and thus prevent the release of the hammer.

(2) When the bullet passes the gas port some of the powder gases pass through the port in the barrel into the cylinder where they strike the piston and then escape through the cylinder port. The piston is driven sharply to the rear about ¼ inch, where its motion is stopped by the gas cylinder nut. The sharp rearward motion of the piston is transmitted by contact to the operating slide, driving it to the rear. The rearward movement of the slide compresses the operating spring.

(3) The initial movement of the operating slide to the rear for about ⅜ inch is independent of the bolt mechanism, the operating lug on the bolt merely sliding in the straight section of the recess in the operating slide. The cam surface in this recess then comes in contact with the operating lug of the bolt and cams it upward rotating the bolt counterclockwise and disengaging the locking lugs on the bolt from their recesses in the receiver. The delay between the initial movement of the operating slide and the unlocking of the bolt enables the bullet to leave the muzzle before unlocking begins, thus relieving the pressure in the barrel before the bolt is opened. The rotation of the bolt also cams the hammer back from the base of the firing pin and withdraws the point of the firing pin into the bolt.

(4) As the operating slide continues its movement to the rear, it carries with it the bolt which slides along the receiver. The empty cartridge case is withdrawn from the chamber

by the extractor (fig. 11). When the mouth of the empty cartridge case clears the breech, the ejector, which is continually pressing on the base of the cartridge, ejects the empty case to the right front through the action of the ejector spring. While the bolt is moving rearward, its rear end bears against the hammer and forces it back and down, thus compressing the hammer spring. The bolt finally loses its rearward motion near the rear end of the receiver. With the bolt at its extreme rearward position, the magazine is uncovered. The magazine follower, actuated by the magazine spring, forces the cartridges upward in the magazine so that the top cartridge lies in the path of the bolt. The rearward movement of the operating slide terminates when

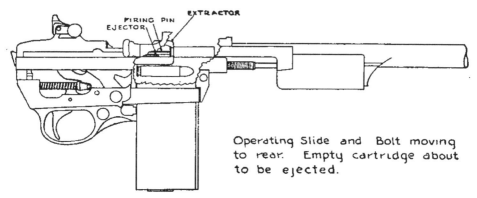

Operating Slide and Bolt moving to rear. Empty cartridge about to be ejected.

FIGURE 11.—Operating slide and bolt moving to rear.

the rear end of the sleeve section contacts the front face of the receiver.

b. Forward movement.—(1) As the bolt moves forward, actuated by the compressed operating slide spring, the lower front face of the bolt comes in contact with the base of the top cartridge and slides it forward into the chamber (see fig. 12). The hammer, under pressure from the hammer spring, rides on the bottom of the bolt and tends to follow it, but is caught and held by the front end of the sear, which engages in the rear notch on the hammer. When pressure on the trigger is released, the hammer spring imparts a slight forward motion to the hammer, which pivots just enough to push the sear slightly backward and cause its rear end to ride over the trigger lip, completing the cocking action. If, however, the pressure on the trigger has *not* been released, that is, if the trigger is held back after firing, the rear end of the sear cannot rise above the trigger lip, and the cocking action cannot be completed.

(2) When the bolt approaches its forward position the rim of the cartridge is engaged by the extractor, and the base of the cartridge forces the ejector into the bolt, thus compressing the ejector spring. The operating lug on the bolt is cammed downward by the rear surface of the cam recess in the operating slide, and in this manner the operating slide rotates the bolt clockwise to engage the locking lugs in the receiver. This action locks the bolt. The operating slide then continues to move forward for about $\frac{5}{16}$ inch until the

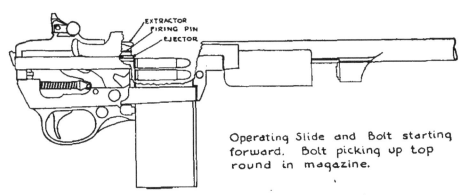

Operating Slide and Bolt starting forward. Bolt picking up top round in magazine.

FIGURE 12.—Start of forward movement.

rear end of the straight section of the recess in the operating slide contacts the operating lug on the bolt. The carbine is now ready to be fired again.

(3) The cycle described in (1) and (2) above is repeated each time the trigger is squeezed until the magazine is empty.

SECTION V

OPERATION

■ 21. WHEN TAKEN UP.—The operation of the carbine will be taken up at any convenient time after instruction in care and cleaning has been completed.

■ 22. To Load Magazine.—Insert 15 rounds in the magazine so that the base of each cartridge is close to the rear wall of the magazine and all cartridges are properly alined.

■ 23. To Load Carbine.—The operation of loading is performed with the piece locked, that is, with the safety of the piece pushed to the right, except in sustained firing. Hold the carbine with the left hand just in front of the magazine opening. With the right hand insert a fully loaded magazine in the magazine opening, making sure that it snaps into place. With the forefinger of the right hand, pull the operating slide smartly all the way back and release it, closing the bolt. The closing of the bolt may be assisted by a push forward on the operating slide handle with the heel of the right hand.

■ 24. To Unload Carbine.—The operation of unloading is also performed with the piece locked. Hold the carbine at the small of the stock with the right hand. Press the magazine lock to the left with the forefinger of the right hand, and at the same time withdraw the magazine from the receiver with the left hand, taking care that it does not drop on a hard surface and suffer damage. With the forefinger of the right hand, pull the operating slide all the way back noting that a cartridge or empty cartridge case is ejected. If nothing is ejected, glance into the chamber to see that it is empty. Ease the operating slide forward gently. *CAUTION: Note that removal of magazine does not unload carbine.*

■ 25. To Operate Carbine as Single Loader.—Making sure the receiver is empty, pull the operating slide to the rear and press down on the operating slide catch with the right thumb, locking the operating slide in its rear position. With the thumb and forefinger of the right hand, insert a single cartridge into the chamber. Pull back on the operating slide handle and release it allowing the bolt to go forward.

■ 26. To Fire Carbine.—With the right thumb push the safety from right to left into the off position. Squeeze the trigger for each shot, releasing the pressure on the trigger between shots.

■ 27. To Set Carbine at Safe.—The loaded carbine will be kept locked until the moment for firing. To lock the carbine push the safety from left to right. In this position the trigger cannot be pulled as the safety locks the sear into the sear notch on the hammer. The carbine may be loaded and operated by hand when locked but cannot be fired. To unlock the carbine, push the safety from right to left with the right thumb.

■ 28. Safety Precautions.—The soldier must be impressed with the fact that while any cartridges remain in the receiver after a round has been fired, the carbine is ready to fire. The gun is safe only when it is cleared; in other words, the gun is *never safe* when the bolt is closed.

■ 29. To Clear Carbine.—*a.* To clear the carbine, unload it as in paragraph 24. Engage the operating slide catch in its indent in the receiver. Glance into the chamber to see that it is empty. *Leave the bolt open.*

b. In range firing, execute clear carbine whenever firing ceases.

Section VI

IMMEDIATE ACTION AND STOPPAGES

■ 30. When Taken Up.—Instruction in immediate action and stoppages will be completed before any firing is done by the individual.

■ 31. Immediate Action.—*a. General.*—Immediate action is the unhesitating application of a probable remedy for a stoppage. It deals with methods of reducing stoppages and not causes. It is taught as an unhesitating manual operation applied to reduce stoppages without detailed consideration of their causes.

b. Procedure.—(1) *Carbine fails to fire.*—With the right hand palm up, use the little finger to pull the operating slide to the rear. Release the operating rod, and if the operating slide goes fully home, aim and fire. To avoid injury in case of hangfire, the hand is so held that no part of the palm or wrist can be struck by the operating slide in its rapid rearward movement.

(2) *Bolt cannot be locked.*—If after following the procedure prescribed in (1) above, the bolt does not go completely forward and lock, again pull operating handle to the rear. Check for a battered round, dirt or obstruction on the face of the bolt, in the chamber, or in the locking recess. Discard the battered round; remove the obstruction. Release the operating slide handle, aim, and fire.

(3) *Bolt locks but carbine again fails to fire.*—If after procedure prescribed in (1) above, the bolt locks and the carbine still does not fire, again pull operating handle to the rear. If no cartridge is ejected, reduce obstruction in magazine by pressing and rotating the upper cartridges. Release the operating slide handle, aim, and fire.

(4) *Carbine fails to feed.*—Keep carbine in action by manually working operating slide. A detailed examination for the malfunction may be made later when time permits.

c. *Detailed examination.*—The above procedure of immediate action will almost invariably keep the carbine in action. In case this immediate action is not successful, a more detailed examination for the possible malfunctions listed in paragraph 32e may be made as circumstances permit.

■ 32. STOPPAGES.—a. *General.*—While immediate action and stoppages are closely related as to subject matter, the former is treated separately to emphasize its importance as an automatic and definite procedure to be applied to overcome stoppages. Proper care of the carbine before, during, and after firing will usually eliminate stoppages. Stoppages which cannot be remedied by the application of immediate action can best be eliminated if the soldier has an understanding of the functioning of the weapon and the causes of stoppages.

b. *Failure to fire.*—(1) *Causes.*—Failure to fire is generally caused by—

(a) Defective ammunition.

(b) Defective firing pin,

(c) Bolt not fully closed when hammer strikes firing pin.

(2) *Action.*—If the primer of a round is deeply indented, the round is defective. Discard the round. If the primer is not indented or is lightly indented, the firing pin may be short or broken, or the bolt may not have been fully closed.

24

Check for dirt or some obstruction which does not permit the bolt to lock fully. Remove the obstruction. If the carbine is clean and lubricated, check the firing pin. Replace it if defective. As the disassembly of the bolt requires special tools, replacement of the firing pin should be made by specialists or ordnance personnel.

c. *Failure to feed.*—(1) *Types.*—Failure to feed is caused by the bolt not going far enough to the rear to pick up a new round. A failure to feed may have a number of causes and results generally in one of the following types of stoppages:

(a) That in which the bolt fails to go fully home.

(b) That in which the bolt does go fully home.

(2) *Action to reduce stoppage of these types.*—Stoppages of the first type may be caused by a battered round, dirt in the locking recesses, an obstruction on the face of the bolt, a dirty chamber, or a ruptured cartridge case, part of which remains in the chamber. Remove the battered round, dirt, or other obstruction; clean the chamber; or remove the ruptured cartridge case. Sometimes this stoppage may be caused by a magazine which has lost its spring tension and does not hold the cartridge firmly in line. Occasionally, when a stoppage of the second type occurs, the spent case is not ejected but is re-fed into the chamber. This condition is caused by lack of lubrication, excessive friction of the moving parts, or lack of sufficient gas pressure due to formation of carbon in the gas port. In any event the bolt has not moved far enough to the rear to permit proper functioning.

d. *Failure to extract.*—(1) *Causes.*—Failures to extract are generally caused by—

(a) Extremely dirty chamber.

(b) Extremely dirty ammunition.

(c) Improper assembly of the carbine, that is, failure to replace the extractor plunger and spring.

(d) Cartridge case chambered in a hot barrel.

(e) Broken extractor.

(2) *Action.*—(a) When a failure to extract occurs, the bolt may be found fully locked with a spent case in the chamber. Generally, most failures to extract can be remedied by pushing the operating slide fully forward and then pulling

it smartly to the rear. If this does not remove the case, use the cleaning rod.

(b) Sometimes the empty case will be left in the chamber, the extractor ripping through the base of the cartridge. When this occurs the bolt generally will attempt to feed a fresh cartridge into the chamber. It will then be necessary to remove this round before the spent case can be removed.

(c) When the chamber or ammunition is dirty, clean the chamber and discard or wipe off the ammunition. Faulty assembly or a broken extractor will cause recurring failures to extract. Replace missing or broken parts.

e. *Table of stoppages.*—The following table may be found of value. It includes the stoppages outlined above and others which have not been covered but which may occur occasionally.

TABLE OF STOPPAGES

Malfunction	Cause	Correction by the soldier or ordnance personnel
Failure to extract_____	Dirty or rough chamber____	Clean chamber.
Failure to feed_____	(1) Dirty or rough chamber_	(1) Clean chamber.
	(2) Restricted gas port_____	(2) Clean gas port.
	(3) Dirty or improperly lubricated carbine.	(3) Clean carbine and lubricate.
	(4) Damaged magazine_____	(4) Replace magazine.
	(5) Ruptured cartridge case in chamber.	(5) Remove ruptured cartridge case.
	(6) Magazine not fully home_	(6) Push magazine home.
Fires automatically___	Sear broken or remains in open position.	Replace trigger group assembly or sear.
Safety releases when pressure is applied on trigger.	Round heel on safety, or broken safety.	Replace safety.
Pull on trigger does not release hammer.	Deformed hammer or trigger, or worn trigger pin.	Replace defective part.
Hammer releases but gun does not fire.	(1) Bolt not all the way seated.	(1) Clean and lubricate.
	(2) Defective ammunition.	(2) Discard round.
	(3) Broken firing pin.	(3) Replace.

f. *Other stoppages.*—In the event of stoppages that are not mentioned above and cannot be reduced, the carbine should be turned in for examination and repair.

SECTION VII

SPARE PARTS AND ACCESSORIES

■ 33. SPARE PARTS.—*a.* The parts of any carbine will in time become unserviceable through breakage or wear resulting from continuous usage. For this reason spare parts are supplied. These are extra parts provided with the carbine for replacement of the parts most likely to fail, for use in making minor repairs, and for general care of the carbine. They should be kept clean and lightly oiled to prevent rust. Sets of spare parts should be kept complete at all times. Whenever a spare part is used to replace a defective part in the rifle, the defective part should be repaired or a new one substituted in the spare part set as soon as possible. Parts that are carried complete should at all times be correctly assembled and ready for immediate insertion in the carbine. The allowance of spare parts for the carbine is prescribed in SNL B–28.

b. With the exception of replacements with the spare parts referred to in *a* above, repairs or alterations to the carbine by using organizations are prohibited.

■ 34. ACCESSORIES.—*a. General.*—Accessories include the tools required for assembling and disassembling and for the cleaning of the carbine, the gun sling, spare parts containers, covers, arm locker, etc. Accessories should not be used for purposes other than those for which they are intended. When not in use they should be stored in the places or receptacles provided for them.

b. Arm locker and rack.—The arm locker and the arm rack are used to store or stack carbines to prevent mishandling or pilfering.

c. Cleaning rod and cleaning brush.—The cleaning rod has a handle at one end and is threaded at the other end to receive the patch section or the brush. This rod is of the correct length to prevent damaging the face of the bolt. The cleaning brush is used to clean the bore of the carbine.

d. Gun sling.—The gun sling, fastened to the swivels of the carbine, is adjusted to suit the particular soldier using it. The sling consists of a long web strap, which may be lengthened or shortened as desired. The sling is furnished to provide the soldier with a means of carrying the carbine. It is not needed in firing.

e. Ruptured-cartridge extractor.—The ruptured-cartridge extractor has the general form of a caliber .30 carbine cartridge. It consists of three parts: the spindle; the head; and the sleeve. The ruptured-cartridge extractor is inserted through the ruptured opening of the case and pushed forward into the chamber. The bolt is let forward without excessive shock so that the extractor of the carbine engages the head of the ruptured-cartridge extractor. As the operating slide is drawn back, the ruptured-cartridge extractor, holding the cartridge on its sleeve, is extracted.

f. Oiler.—The oiler consists of a tube to hold lubricating oil, a steel ring or cap seat and a threaded cap in which is positioned a rod or dropper. The oiler also acts as an anchor pin for the sling.

g. Cleaning rod case.—This fabric container is sewed in five pockets to hold the cleaning brush and the four sections of the cleaning rod.

SECTION VIII

AMMUNITION

■ 35. LOT NUMBER.—When ammunition is manufactured, an ammunition lot number is assigned which becomes an essential part of the marking in accordance with specifications. This lot number is marked on all packing containers and the identification card inclosed in each packing box. It is required for all purposes of record, including grading and use, reports on condition, functioning, and accidents in which the ammunition might be involved. Only those lots of grades appropriate for the weapon will be fired. Since it is impracticable to mark the ammunition lot number on each cartridge, every effort should be made to maintain the ammunition lot number with the cartridges once the cartridges are removed from the original packing. Cartridges which have been removed from the original packing and for which the ammunition lot number has been lost are placed in grade 3. It is, therefore, obvious that when cartridges are removed from their original packings they should be so marked that the ammunition lot number is preserved.

■ 36. GRADE.—Current grades of all existing lots of small arms ammunition are established by the Chief of Ordnance and are published in ordnance field service bulletins. No lot other than one approved by the Ordnance Department will be fired.

■ 37. CARE, HANDLING, AND PRESERVATION.—*a.* Small arms ammunition is not dangerous to handle. Care, however, must be taken not to break or damage the boxes. All broken boxes must be immediately repaired, and all markings transferred to the new parts of the box.

b. The ammunition comes in boxes of 2,000 rounds, packed in 40 cartons of 50 rounds each. Ammunition boxes should

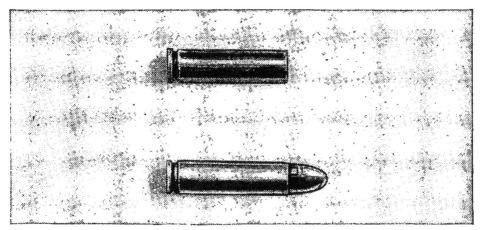

FIGURE 13.—Cartridge and cartridge case, carbine, caliber .30, M1.

not be opened until the ammunition is needed. Ammunition removed from containers, particularly in damp climates, may corrode and thereby become unserviceable.

c. The ammunition should be protected from mud, sand, dirt, and water. If it gets wet or dirty, wipe it off at once. Light corrosion should be wiped off. Cartridges should not be polished to make them look brighter.

d. No carbine ammunition will be fired until it has been positively identified by ammunition lot number and grade.

■ 38. CARTRIDGE, CARBINE, CALIBER .30, M1.—The approximate maximum range for the cartridge is 2,000 yards. Its muzzle velocity is 1,900 feet per second. It is illustrated in figure 13.

SECTION IX

INDIVIDUAL SAFETY PRECAUTIONS

■ 39. RULES.—*a.* Consider every carbine to be loaded until it has been examined and proved to be unloaded. Never trust your memory as to its condition in this respect.

b. Never point the carbine at anyone you do not intend to shoot, nor in a direction where an accidental discharge may do harm.

c. Always unload the carbine if it is to be left where someone else may handle it.

d. Always point the carbine up when snapping the trigger after examination.

e. If it is desired to carry the piece cocked with a cartridge in the chamber, the bolt mechanism will be secured by turning the safety lock to the right.

f. Under no circumstances should the firing pin be let down by hand on a cartridge in the chamber.

g. Never fire a carbine with any grease, cleaning patch, dust, dirt, mud, snow, or other obstruction in the bore. To do so may burst the barrel.

h. Never grease or oil the ammunition or the walls of the carbine chamber. This creates a hazardous pressure on the carbine bolt.

i. See that the ammunition is clean and dry. Examine all live and dummy ammunition. Turn in all cartridges with loose bullets or which appear to be otherwise defective.

j. Do not allow the ammunition to be exposed to the direct rays of the sun for any length of time. This creates hazardous chamber pressures.

CHAPTER 2

MARKSMANSHIP—KNOWN-DISTANCE TARGETS

SECTION I

GENERAL

■ 40. PURPOSE.—The purpose of this chapter is to provide a thorough and uniform method of training individuals to be good carbine shots and of testing their proficiency in firing at known-distance targets.

■ 41. NECESSITY FOR TRAINING.—*a.* Without proper training a man instinctively does the wrong thing in firing the carbine. He gives the trigger a sudden pressure which causes flinching. However, if he is thoroughly instructed and drilled in the mechanism of correct shooting, and is then carefully and properly coached when he begins firing, he rapidly acquires correct shooting habits.

b. Carbine firing is a mechanical operation which anyone who is physically and mentally fit to be a soldier can learn to do well if properly instructed. The methods of instruction are the same as those used in teaching any mechanical operation. The training is divided into steps which must be taught in proper sequence. The soldier is carefully coached and is corrected whenever he starts to make a mistake.

■ 42. FUNDAMENTALS.—To become a good carbine shot the soldier must be thoroughly trained in the following essentials of good shooting:

a. Correct sighting and aiming.

b. Correct positions.

31

c. Correct trigger squeeze.

d. Correct application of rapid fire principles.

e. Knowledge of proper sight adjustments.

■ 43. PHASES OF TRAINING.—*a.* Marksmanship training is divided into two phases:

(1) Preparatory marksmanship training.

(2) Range practice.

b. No soldier should be given range practice until he has had a thorough course of preparatory training.

c. The soldier should be proficient in mechanical training and related subjects before he receives marksmanship training.

d. Every man who is to fire on the range will be put through the entire preparatory course. No distinction will be made between recruits and men who have had range practice, regardless of their previous qualification. Some part of the preparatory instruction may have escaped them in previous years; it is certain that some of it has been forgotten, and in any case it will be helpful to go over it again and refresh the mind on the subject.

e. All of the noncommissioned officers and other men selected as assistant instructors and special coaches of the unit will be put through a course of instruction and required to pass a rigid test before being used as instructors.

■ 44. RECRUIT INSTRUCTION.—As a part of their recruit training, all recruits armed with the carbine will be given thorough mechanical training and instructed in the fundamental elements of carbine marksmanship—sighting and aiming, positions, trigger squeeze, and rapid fire. Instruction in carbine marksmanship will commence with the initial instruction of the recruit and will continue throughout the period of recruit training.

■ 45. LEADERS AND COMMANDERS—DUTIES AND EQUIPMENT.—*a. General.*—In units where relatively small numbers of men are armed with the carbine, it may be found desirable both for instruction purposes and for range practice to assemble the carbineers in each battalion into a provisional company. Well-qualified instructors should be attached to the provisional company by the battalion commander.

b. Duties.—(1) *Squad leader.*—(a) Organizes the work in his squad so that each man is occupied during the preparatory period in the prescribed form of training for target practice.

(*b*) Tests each man in his squad at the end of the training on each preparatory step and assigns him a mark in the proper place on the blank form showing state of training.

(*c*) Sees that each man takes proper care of his carbine and that he cleans it at the end of each day's firing.

(*d*) Requires correct aiming, correct positions, and proper trigger squeeze when fire is simulated in drills and maneuvers.

(2) *Platoon leader.*—Supervises and directs the squad leaders in training their squads; personally checks each man in his platoon on the points enumerated on the blank form; and examines each man generally along the lines outlined in paragraph 53.

(3) *Company commander.*—R e q u i r e s the prescribed methods of instruction and coaching to be carried out in detail; supervises and directs the squad and platoon leaders; in companies of less than 60 men performs the duties prescribed for platoon leaders in (2) above.

(4) *Battalion commander.*—Sees that his instructors know the prescribed methods of instruction and coaching; supervises the instruction of his battalion and requires his instructors to follow the preparatory exercises and methods of coaching in detail.

c. Equipment.—All equipment used in the preparatory exercises must be accurately and carefully made. One of the objects of these exercises is to cultivate a sense of exactness and carefulness in the minds of the men undergoing instruction. They cannot be exact with inexact instruments, and they will not be careful when working with equipment that is carelessly made.

SECTION II

PREPARATORY MARKSMANSHIP TRAINING

■ 46. GENERAL.—*a.* The purpose of preparatory marksmanship training is to teach the soldier the essentials of good shooting, and to develop fixed and correct shooting habits before he undertakes range practice.

b. Preparatory marksmanship training is divided into the six following steps and should be concentrated in the period of time allotted:

(1) Sighting and aiming exercises.

(2) Position exercises.

(3) Trigger-squeeze exercises.

(4) Rapid-fire exercises.

(5) Instruction in the effect of wind, in sight changes, and in the use of the score book.

(6) Examination of men before starting range practice.

c. Each step is divided into exercises designed to teach the soldier the importance of each operation and to drill him in those operations until he is able to execute them correctly.

d. Instruction in the effect of wind, sight changes, and the use of the score book can be taught indoors during inclement weather. It is not a training step that need be given in any particular sequence but it must be covered prior to the examination. The first four steps are taught in the order listed; each one involves the technique learned in the preceding steps.

e. Each of the first four steps starts with a lecture by the instructor to the assembled group. This lecture includes a demonstration by a squad which the instructor puts through the exercises that are to constitute the day's work. He shows exactly how to do the exercises that are to be taken up and explains why they are done and their application to carbine shooting. He shows how the squad leader organizes the work so that no men are idle, and how they coach each other when they are not under instruction by an officer or noncommissioned officer. These talks and demonstrations are an essential part of the training. If properly given they awaken the interest and enthusiasm of the whole command for the work and give an exact knowledge of how each step is to be carried on—something that men cannot get from reading a description, no matter how accurate and detailed that description may be. The instructor who gives these talks and demonstrations may be the platoon leader of his platoon, the company commander of his company, or the battalion commander of his battalion; or he may be a specially qualified officer who has been detailed as officer in charge of carbine instruction.

f. The form below shows the state of instruction and should be kept by each squad leader and by each platoon leader independently of his squad leaders.

Name	Care and cleaning of the carbine	Sighting bar	Sighting and aiming with carbine	Shot group exercises	Blackening sights	Taking up the slack	Holding the breath	Positions	Assuming positions rapidly	Trigger squeeze	Calling the shot	Rapid fire	Sight changes	Effect of light and wind	Use of score book	Ability to coach	Final examination

METHOD OF MARKING

Fair:
```
X
```
Good:
```
  X
    X
```
Excellent:
```
  X
    X
      X
```
Excellent and has instructional ability:
```
  X
    X
  X   X
```

g. The instruction must be thorough and it must be individual. Each man must understand every point and be able to explain each one in his own words. The company commander carefully supervises the work. He should pick out men at random from time to time and put them through a test to see if the instruction is thorough and is progressing satisfactorily.

h. Interest and enthusiasm must be sustained. If these exercises become perfunctory, they do more harm than good.

i. Careful attention must be paid to the essential points covered in the questions and answers in paragraph 53. Instructors will consult these during each step of the preparatory work. Each man must be tested thoroughly before he is allowed to fire.

j. The coach-and-pupil system is used during the preparatory exercises, whenever a man is in a firing position. The men are grouped in pairs and take turns in coaching each other. The man giving instruction is called the coach. The man undergoing instruction is called the pupil. When the men of a pair change places, the pupil becomes the coach and the coach becomes the pupil.

k. Correct shooting habits should be acquired during the preparatory training period. All errors must be noted, brought to the attention of the pupil, and corrected. Each soldier must be impressed with the importance of exactness in every detail. For example, there is no such thing as a trigger squeeze that is "about right"; it is either perfect or it is wrong.

■ 47. BLACKENING SIGHTS.—In all preparatory exercises involving aiming, and in all range firing, both sights of the carbine should be blackened. Before blackening the sights, they should be cleaned and all traces of oil removed. The blackening is done by holding each sight for a few seconds in the point of a small flame so that a uniform coating of lampblack will be deposited on the metal. Materials commonly used for this purpose are carbide lamp, cylinder of carbide gas, kerosene lamp, candles and small pine sticks. Shoe paste may also be used.

■ 48. FIRST STEP—SIGHTING AND AIMING.—*a. First exercise.*— The instructor shows a sighting bar (fig. 14) to his group and explains its use as follows:

(1) The front and rear sights on the sighting bar represent enlarged carbine sights.

(2) The sighting bar is used in the first sighting and aiming exercise because with it small errors can be seen easily and explained to the pupil.

(3) The eyepiece requires the pupil to place his eye in such a position that he sees the sights in exactly the same alinement as seen by the coach.

(4) There is no eyepiece on the carbine, but the pupil learns by use of the sighting bar how to aline the sights when using the carbine.

(5) Attaching the removable target to the end of the sight-

ing bar is a simple method of readily alining the sights on a bull's-eye.

(6) The instructor explains the peep sight to the assembled group and shows each man the illustrations of a correct sight alinement (fig. 15).

(7) With the target removed, the instructor adjusts the sights of the sighting bar to illustrate a correct alinement of the sights. Each man of the assembled group looks through the eyepiece at the sight adjustments.

(8) He then adjusts the sights of the sighting bar with various small errors in alinement and has each man try to detect the error.

(9) The instructor describes a correct aim, showing the illustration to each man. He explains that the top of the

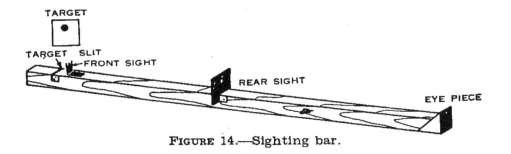

FIGURE 14.—Sighting bar.

front sight is seen through the middle of the circle and just touches the bottom of the bull's-eye, so that all the bull's-eye can be clearly seen (fig. 15).

(10) The eye should be focused on the bull's-eye in aiming, and the instructor assures himself, by questioning the men, that each understands what is meant by focusing the eye on the bull's-eye.

(11) The instructor adjusts the sights of the sighting bar and the removable target so as to illustrate a correct aim and requires each man of the group to look through the eyepiece to observe the correct aim.

(12) He adjusts the sights and the removable target of the sighting bar so as to illustrate various small errors and requires each man in the group to attempt to detect the error.

(13) The exercise described above having been completed by the squad leader or other instructor, the men are placed

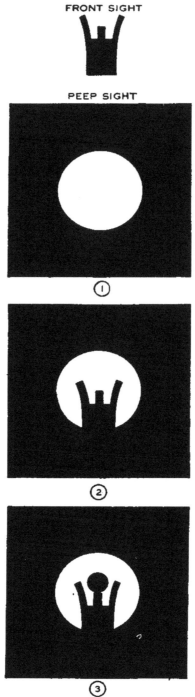

FIGURE 15.—Sight alinement.

in pairs and repeat the exercise by the coach-and-pupil method.

(14) As soon as the pupil is considered proficient in the first sighting and aiming exercise, he is put through the second and third sighting and aiming exercises by the instructor. Such pupils are then placed in pairs to instruct each other in these two exercises by the coach-and-pupil method.

b. Second exercise.—(1) A carbine with sights blackened is placed in a carbine rest (fig. 16①) and pointed at a blank sheet of paper mounted on a box. Without touching the carbine or the carbine rest, the coach takes the position illustrated and looks through the sights (fig. 16① and ②). The coach directs the marker by command or signal to move the small disk until the bottom of the bull's-eye is in correct alinement with the sights and then commands: HOLD, to the marker. The coach moves away from the carbine and directs the pupil to look through the sights in order to observe the correct aim.

(2) After the pupil has observed the correct aim, the marker moves the disk out of alinement. The pupil then takes position and directs the marker to move the disk until the bottom of the bull's-eye is in correct alinement with the sights. The coach then looks through the sights to see if the alinement is correct.

(3) The coach alines the sights on the bull's-eye with various slight errors to determine whether or not the pupil can detect them.

c. Third exercise.—(1) The object of this exercise is to show the importance of uniform and correct aiming, and to foster a sense of exactness. At 50 feet and with a small bull's-eye a man should be able to place all three marks so that they can be covered by the unsharpened end of a lead pencil.

(2) This exercise is conducted as follows: The carbine with the sights blackened is placed in a carbine rest and pointed at a blank sheet of paper mounted on a box. The pupil takes the position illustrated and looks through the sights without touching the carbine or carbine rest. The pupil directs the marker to move the disk until the bottom of the bull's-eye is in correct alinement with the sights, and then commands:

HOLD, to the marker. The coach then looks through the sights to see if the alinement is correct. Without saying anything to the pupil, he commands: MARK, to the marker. The marker, without moving the disk, makes a dot on the paper with a sharp-pointed pencil inserted through the hole in the center of the bull's-eye. The marker then moves the disk to change the alinement. The pupil and coach without touching the carbine or carbine rest repeat this operation until three dots, numbered 1, 2, 3, respectively, have been made. These dots outline the shot group, and the pupil's name is written under it. The size and shape of the shot

FIGURE 16.—Position for second sighting and aiming exercise.

group are then discussed and the errors pointed out. This exercise is repeated until proficiency is attained.

(3) This exercise should also be practiced at 100 yards and 200 yards on a 10-inch movable bull's-eye. These shot group exercises at longer ranges teach the men to aim accurately at a distant target, the outlines of which are indistinct. At 100 yards a man should be able to make a shot group that can be covered with a half dollar, and at 200 yards one that can be covered with a dollar.

(4) Tissue paper may be used to trace each man's shot group at the longer ranges. The name of the pupil is written on the tissue paper under the shot group he made. These tracings are sent back to the firing line so that the pupil can see what he has done.

(5) The third sighting and aiming exercise, especially the

②

FIGURE 16.—Position for second sighting and aiming exercise.—Continued.

200-yard shot group work, is continued during the time devoted to the second and third preparatory steps. The reason for continuing this exercise is to bring backward men up to the required state of proficiency and to maintain interest (fig. 17).

(6) Competition between the individuals of a squad to see which one can make the smallest shot group is valuable in creating and maintaining interest.

■ 49. SECOND STEP—POSITIONS.—*a. General.*—Instruction in position with the carbine includes taking up the slack, holding the breath, and aiming.

b. Taking up the slack.—The first movement of the trigger which takes place when light pressure is applied is called *taking up the slack.* It is part of the position exercise because this play must be taken up by the finger as soon as the correct position is assumed and before careful aiming is begun. The entire amount of slack in the trigger is taken up by one positive movement of the finger.

c. Holding the breath.—(1) Holding the breath in the proper manner while aiming is very important. It will be found that a large proportion of men in any group undergoing instruction in carbine marksmanship do not know how to hold the breath in the proper manner. Each man must be carefully instructed and tested on this point. The correct manner of holding the breath must be practiced at all times during position and trigger-squeeze exercises and whenever firing or simulating fire.

(2) To hold the breath properly, draw into the lungs a little more air than is used in an ordinary breath. Let out a little of this air and stop the remainder by closing the throat so that the air remaining in the lungs will press against the closed throat. Do not hold the breath with the throat open or by the muscular action of the diaphram as if attempting to draw in more air. The important point is to be comfortable and steady while aiming and squeezing the trigger.

d. Aiming.—The carbine is carefully aimed at a target each time a firing position is assumed.

e. General rules for positions.—The general rules which follow are common to the prone, sitting, kneeling, and stand-

FIGURE 17.—Position for third sighting and aiming exercise on long ranges (distance foreshortened).

Ing positions. The exact details of a position for any individual depend on his conformation.

(1) To assume any position, half face to right and then assume the position.

(2) In assuming any position there is some point at which the carbine points naturally and without effort. If this point is not the center of the target, the whole body and carbine must be shifted so as to bring the carbine into proper alinement. Otherwise the firer will be firing under a strain because he will be pulling the carbine toward the target by muscular effort for each shot.

(3) The right hand grasps the small of the stock. The right thumb may be either over the small of the stock or on top of the stock; it should not be placed alongside the stock.

(4) The left hand is in rear of the upper band swivel, the hand and wrist joint straight, carbine resting in the crotch formed by the thumb and index finger and resting on the base of the thumb and heel of the palm of the hand.

(5) The left elbow is placed as nearly under the carbine as it can be placed without appreciable effort.

(6) Ordinarily the second joint of the index finger contacts the trigger. The first joint may be used by men the length of whose arm or the size of whose hand is such as to make it difficult to reach the trigger with the second joint, or to whom the first joint of the finger seems more natural and comfortable.

(7) The cheek is pressed firmly against the stock and placed as far forward as possible without strain to bring the eye near the rear sight.

(8) The butt of the carbine is held firmly against the shoulder.

(9) The carbine should not be canted.

(10) Left-handed men who have difficulty with the right-hand position will be allowed to use the left-hand position.

f. Prone position (fig. 18).—(1) In assuming the prone position the body should lie at an angle of about 45° to the line of aim with the spine straight. The exact angle of the body to the line of aim depends upon the conformation of the firer. The legs should be well apart, the inside of the feet flat on the ground, or as nearly so as can be attained

without strain.   Elbows should be well under the body so as
to raise the chest off the ground.   The right hand grasps
the small of the stock.   The left hand is near the upper band
swivel, as far forward as is comfortable and convenient for
the firer, wrist straight, carbine placed in the crotch formed
by the thumb and index finger and resting on the base of
the thumb and heel of the hand.   The cheek should be
firmly pressed against the stock with the eye as close to the
rear sight as possible, without straining the neck muscles.

(2) The exact details of the position will vary, depending
upon the conformation of the firer.   However, the firer must
secure a position that will not be changed by the recoil of the
weapon.   When the correct position has been attained, it
will be found that upon discharge the muzzle will move slightly up and very slightly to the right, and that it will then
settle back close to the original aiming point.

g. *Sitting position* (fig. 19).—(1) The firer sits half-faced
to the right; feet well apart and well braced on the heels which
are dug slightly into the ground; body leaning well forward
from the hips with back straight; both arms resting inside
the legs and well supported; cheek pressed firmly against the
stock and placed as far forward as possible without straining;
left hand near the upper band swivel, wrist straight, carbine
placed in the crotch formed by the thumb and index finger
and resting on the base of the thumb and heel of the hand.

(2) The sitting position is used in the field when firing
from ground that slopes downward to the front.   In practicing this position the feet may be slightly lower than the
ground upon which the soldier sits.   Sitting on a low sandbag
is authorized.

(3) In the event the conformation of the firer is such that
he can not assume the prescribed normal position, such
changes as may be necessary to secure a steady, comfortable
position are authorized.

h. *Kneeling position* (fig. 20).—The firer kneels half-faced
to the right on the right knee, sitting on the right heel; the
left knee bent so that the left lower leg is vertical (as seen
from the front); left arm well under the carbine and resting
on the left knee with the point of the elbow beyond the knee-
cap; right elbow above or at the height of the shoulder;

cheek pressed firmly against the stock and placed as far ·
forward as possible without strain. Sitting on the side of
the foot instead of the heel is authorized.

①

②

FIGURE 18.—Prone position.

i. Standing position (fig. 21).—The firer stands half-faced to the right; feet from 1 foot to 2 feet apart; body erect and

①

②

FIGURE 19.—Sitting position.

well balanced; left elbow well under the carbine; left hand in rear of the upper swivel, wrist straight, carbine placed in the crotch formed by the thumb and index finger and resting on the base of the thumb and the heel of the hand; butt of the piece high up on the shoulder and firmly held; right elbow approximately at the height of the shoulder; cheek pressed against the stock and as far forward as possible without strain. A position with the left hand against or under the trigger guard and with the left upper arm supported against the body is not a practical field position and is prohibited.

FIGURE 20.—Kneeling position.

j. Procedure in conducting position exercises.—(1) Small bull's-eyes are used as aiming points. These bull's-eyes should be placed at a range of 1,000 inches and at different heights so that in aiming from various positions the carbine will be nearly horizontal, or standard targets may be installed at distances of 100, 200, or 300 yards.

(2) Before taking up each phase of the position exercise, the instructor assembles his squad or group, and—

(*a*) Shows them the proper method of blackening the front and rear sights of the carbine and has each pupil blacken his sights.

(*b*) Explains and demonstrates the proper manner of taking up the slack and has each pupil practice it.

(*c*) Explains and demonstrates the proper manner of holding the breath and has each pupil practice it.

(*d*) Explains the general rules which apply to all positions.

(*e*) Explains and demonstrates the different positions.

(3) Following explanations and demonstrations the instruction becomes individual by the coach-and-pupil method.

FIGURE 21.—Standing position.

Each pupil, after seeing that his sights are blackened, takes position, alines his sights, takes up the slack, holds his breath, and perfects the sight picture. As soon as his aim becomes unsteady, the exercise ceases. After a short rest the pupil repeats the exercise without further command. The trigger is not squeezed in the position exercises. Exercises are conducted in all positions.

(4) In the position exercises, it is the duty of the coach to see that—

(a) The sights are blackened.

(b) The proper position is taken.

(c) The slack is taken up promptly.

(d) The pupil aims.

(e) The breath is held while aiming. The coach checks the pupil's manner of holding his breath by watching his back.

■ 50. THIRD STEP—TRIGGER SQUEEZE.—a. *Importance of trigger squeeze.*—(1) The most important item in shooting is to squeeze the trigger in such a way as to fire the carbine without affecting the aim. Misses and poor shots are due to spoiling the aim just before the discharge takes place. This is caused by jerking the trigger and flinching. The trigger must be squeezed so steadily that the firer cannot know the instant the piece will be fired. If a man squeezes the trigger so steadily that he cannot know when the discharge will take place, he does not spoil his aim and he will not flinch, because he does not know when to flinch.

(2) No good shot attempts to discharge the piece the instant his sights are alined on the mark. Instead, he holds his aim as accurately alined on the mark as possible and maintains a steadily increasing pressure upon the trigger until the shot is fired. This method of squeezing the trigger must be carried out in all simulated firing or the value of the practice is lost.

(3) There is only one correct method of squeezing the trigger—a steady increase of pressure so that the firer does not know when the explosion will take place.

(4) Expert shots are men who through training have learned to increase the pressure only when the sights are in correct alinement with the bull's-eye. When the sights become slightly out of alinement, they hold what they have with the finger and only continue the increase of pressure when the sights again become properly alined.

(5) The difference between poor shots and good shots is measured in their ability to squeeze the trigger properly. Any man with fair eyesight and strength can aline the sights on the target and hold them there for an appreciable length

of time. When he has acquired sufficient will power and self-control to forget that there is to be an explosion and a shock, and squeezes the trigger with a steady increase of pressure until the carbine is fired, he has become a good shot, and not until then. This squeeze of the trigger applies to rapid fire as well as slow fire. The increase of pressure is faster in rapid fire, but the process is the same.

b. *Calling the shot.*—The pupil must always notice where the sights are pointed at the instant the carbine is fired, and must call out at once where he thinks the bullet will hit. Shots are called even when simulating fire at a mark, in order to acquire the habit and to develop a closer hold. No man can become a good shot until he is able to call his shot before it is marked. Inability to call a shot indicates the firer did not know where the sights were pointing at the time the carbine was fired; in other words, he shut his eyes first and fired afterward.

c. *Procedure in conducting trigger-squeeze exercises.*—(1) (a) The instructor explains to the assembled squad or group the importance of correct trigger squeeze. He assures himself by questions that each pupil understands what is meant by a *steady increase of pressure,* and that he understands that the increase is only applied when the aim is correct and then by a steady, not by a sudden pressure. The instructor explains the necessity for calling the shot. After the above points have been explained the instruction becomes individual by the coach-and-pupil method supervised by the instructor.

(b). The pupil is first taught the trigger squeeze in the prone position. In this position he can hold steadily and has not the temptation to snap the shot the instant the front sight touches the bull's-eye, as he has in a less steady position. After he has learned the principles of correct trigger squeeze in the prone position, he applies them in the other positions.

(c) A great deal of trigger-squeeze exercise is necessary, but it must be carefully watched and coached. Trigger squeeze exercise that is not along the right lines is worse than none.

(d) Soldiers should not be allowed to simulate fire until

they have been thoroughly instructed in trigger squeeze, and then in all drills and field exercises where fire is simulated they should be cautioned to aim at definite objects and to carry out the correct principles of aiming, squeezing the trigger, and calling the shot.

(2) The instruction is individual by the coach-and-pupil method. Aiming targets similar to those mentioned for the position exercises are used. The exercise is conducted at will as outlined for the position exercises.

d. Duties of the coach.—In the trigger-squeeze exercises the coach sees that—

(1) The sights are blackened.

(2) The proper position is taken.

(3) The slack is taken up promptly.

(4) The pupil aims.

(5) The breath is held while aiming. (He checks the breathing by watching the back of the pupil.)

(6) The trigger is squeezed properly.

(7) The pupil calls the shot.

■ 51. FOURTH STEP—RAPID FIRE.—*a. General.*—All points learned in slow fire are applied in rapid fire. It is especially important that the men understand that the aim and the trigger squeeze are the same as in slow fire. Time is gained by taking position rapidly and by reloading quickly and without fumbling.

b. Timing.—A most important element in rapid fire is the development of correct timing in firing. Correct timing in firing will vary from about 5 seconds per shot for the beginner to about 2 seconds per shot for the experienced man. The development of proper timing in firing rests mainly on the correct position of the firer. The firer's position is not correct unless the sights return automatically to the aiming point after each shot is fired. As soon as the sights come back on the aiming point the firer concentrates on the sight picture and squeezes the trigger quickly. This is repeated for each shot. Through training, accurate fire becomes more and more rapid until the ability to fire 25 or more accurate shots per minute is acquired.

(1) In timing exercises the instructor first assembles his group and explains and demonstrates—

(*a*) The importance of correct position.

(*b*) The importance of correct aiming and keeping the eye on the target while firing.

(*c*) How the coach promptly presses back the operating handle with a sharp motion to cock the piece and then releases the pressure to permit the operating handle to go forward (see fig. 22).

(*d*) Correct trigger squeeze.

(*e*) What is meant by correct timing.

(*f*) How speed in timing is gradually increased as skill is

FIGURE 22.—Coach manipulating operating slide.

acquired, until an approximate rate of one shot every .2 seconds is attained.

(2) Following the above explanation and demonstration by the instructor, timing exercises using the coach-and-pupil method are given in all positions except standing.

c. Taking positions rapidly.—(1) *Prone position* (fig. 23).— (*a*) The movement is described by the numbers for the purpose of instruction in the sequence of the movement. After this sequence is learned the position is taken as one motion.

(*b*) First assume the correct position and aim at the target as explained in paragraph 49*f*. Mark the position of the elbows, rise to the knees and then to the feet, without

①

②

FIGURE 23.—Method of assuming prone position rapidly.

FIGURE 23.—Method of assuming prone position rapidly—Continued.

55

changing the position of either foot.   Grasp the carbine, with the right hand at the small of the stock, and hold the piece with the barrel inclined upward at an angle of about 45°.   This is the *ready* position (fig. 23①).

(c) Being at the READY, to take the prone position rapidly:

1. Bend both knees to the ground (fig. 23②).
2. Let the body fall forward from the waist up; break the fall by placing the left hand about 3 feet in front of the left knee (fig. 23② and ③).
3. Place the right elbow on the ground (fig. 23③).
4. Place the butt of the carbine against .the right shoulder (fig. 23④).
5. Place the left elbow on the ground and at the same time grasp the carbine just below the upper band with the left hand (fig. 23⑤).

(2) *Sitting position* (fig. 24).—(a) To assume the sitting position rapidly, break the fall by placing the right hand on the ground slightly to the right rear of the spot on which to sit.

(b) In practicing for range firing, first sit down and aim at the target in the normal sitting position.   Then mark the position of the heels and the spot on which to sit.   Then at the command READY ON THE FIRING LINE, stand with the heels in the places made for them.   As the target appears, sit down on the spot marked; break the fall with the right hand; grasp the small of the stock with the right hand; and assume the aiming position.

(3) *Kneeling position.*—To assume the kneeling position from standing, first kneel and aim at the target in the normal kneeling position.   Then mark the position of the feet and the right knee.   At the command READY ON THE FIRING LINE, stand with the feet in the places marked for them.   As the target appears, kneel with the right knee on the spot marked, place the butt of the carbine against the shoulder and assume the aiming position (see par. 49*h* and fig. 20).

(4) *Practice required.*—Taking positions rapidly from the standing position should be practiced at will, using the coach-and-pupil system.

d. *Reloading carbine.*—To reload, lower the carbine from the shoulder and press the magazine lock to the left with the forefinger of the right hand and, at the same time, remove the magazine from the receiver with the left hand. Then bring the right hand to the second magazine in the open magazine pouch. At the same time turn the carbine to the left with the left hand, so that the magazine opening in the receiver is to the right. Bring the magazine forward and carefully place it in the magazine slots. Tap the bottom of the magazine to seat it fully home. Load the carbine by pulling the operating slide handle sharply to the rear and releasing it.

e. *Procedure in conducting rapid-fire exercises.*—After the pupil has become properly trained in timing, taking positions rapidly, and reloading, he is given additional practice in all of these points by rapid-fire exercises. The group under instruction is paired off, coach and pupil, and placed on line. Full-sized targets are placed at 100, 200 and 300 yards from the men under instruction, with some simple arrangement to permit the targets to be exposed to view for the prescribed period of time. Rapid fire exercises may be conducted at shorter ranges using targets proportionately reduced in size. Sights are set to correspond to the range being used. The commands and procedure are exactly the same as for rapid fire on the range except that firing is simulated. For example, the pupil stands with sights properly set and blackened, and with two empty magazines in the magazine pouch or pocket of his belt. The instructor, after announcing the range, the position to be used, the number of rounds to simulate firing at each target from each position, commands: 1. SIMULATE LOAD AND LOCK, 2. READY ON THE RIGHT, 3. READY ON THE LEFT, 4. READY ON THE FIRING LINE, 5. CEASE FIRING, 6. UNLOAD. At the first command, magazines are inserted, loading simulated, and carbines locked. At the fourth command the safety on all carbines is pushed to the left. When the targets are exposed the pupil assumes the firing position and simulates firing the prescribed number of rounds on the indicated target center, assumes position rapidly, releases the magazine, inserts the second magazine, and simulates loading and firing the prescribed number of rounds at the other target center. Accuracy must not be sacrificed for rapidity. Upon completion of the exercise the bolt is opened.

57

FIGURE 24.—Method of assuming sitting position rapidly.

③

④

FIGURE 24.—Method of assuming sitting position rapidly—Continued.

During simulated firing the pupil should never take his eye from the target except to change position and to simulate reloading. He should count his shots as he fires in order to know when to take the next position and when to reload. The exercise is conducted from the standing firing position to kneeling and sitting firing positions, and from the standing position to the prone position (see par. 55).

f. Duties of coach.—In rapid-fire exercises the coach sees that—

(1) The sights are set for the range designated and are blackened.

(2) The correct position is taken.

(3) The slack is taken up promptly.

(4) The breath is held while aiming.

(5) The trigger is squeezed properly.

(6) The firer simulates firing the prescribed number of shots on each target. (Each time the pupil squeezes the trigger, the coach promptly presses back the operating handle with a sharp motion and then releases the pressure to permit the operating rod handle to go forward.)

(7) The shots of the first magazine are counted.

(8) The firer assumes next position rapidly and correctly.

(9) The firer simulates reloading correctly.

(10) The eye is kept on the target, the elbows kept in place, and the butt of the carbine kept to the shoulder except when reloading.

(11) The carbine is reloaded quickly and without fumbling.

■ 52. FIFTH STEP—EFFECT OF WIND; SIGHT CHANGES; USE OF SCORE BOOK.—*a. Wind.*—(1) In firing at 300 yards or under, the effect of the weather conditions (except that of the wind) on the bullet can be disregarded. The influence of wind must be carefully studied.

(2) The horizontal clock system is used in describing the direction of the wind. The firer is considered at the center of the clock, and the target is at 12 o'clock. A 3 o'clock wind comes directly from the right. A 6 o'clock wind comes straight from the rear. A 9 o'clock wind comes directly from the left. A wind that is constantly changing its direction back and forth is called a "fishtail wind."

(3) The force of the wind is described in miles per hour

and is estimated by throwing up light, dry grass, dust, or light paper and watching how fast it travels, and by observing the danger flags. In general, a light breeze is a 5- to 8-mile wind; a fairly strong breeze is a 10- to 12-mile wind. Wind blowing 20 miles an hour is very strong.

(4) Wind from either side blows the bullet out of its path. Thus, a wind coming from the right° of the firer is blowing on the right side of the bullet and will deflect it to the left. Therefore instead of hitting the bull's-eye it will strike to the left of the bull's-eye (see note below). Correction for this deflection, if using a carbine equipped with the L-sight, should be made by moving the aiming point toward the wind. This is called "taking windage," and is accomplished by shifting the body so that the sights of the carbine, instead of being pointed naturally on the normal point of aim, that is, the bottom of the bull's-eye, will be directed to the right or left of the bull's-eye, depending on the wind. If the standard sight is used, the correction for this deflection is made by applying proper windage to the rear sight. The worst kind of wind in which to shoot is a fishtail wind varying in direction from 11 to 1 o'clock or from 7 to 5 o'clock. The amount the bullet will be blown from its path depends on the force and direction of the wind and on the distance to the target.

NOTE.—Initially, the carbine will be issued equipped with the L-sight. This being a fixed sight, allowance for the effect of wind must be made by aiming the carbine to the right or left as the case may be. The carbine will eventually be fitted with a standard sight that will be adjustable for windage.

(5) The amount of windage to allow for the first shot can be approximately determined by the following rule:

(a) *Wind rule* (approximate only).—The range (expressed in hundreds of yards) squared, multiplied by the velocity of the wind and divided by 5, equals the number of inches to allow for a 3 o'clock or 9 o'clock wind.

(b) *Example.*—At 300 yards the wind is blowing at 10 miles per hour from 3 o'clock; $\dfrac{3 \times 3 \times 10}{5}$ equals 18 inches. Therefore under the conditions stated the aiming point for the first shot would be 18 inches to the right of the normal aiming point.

(6) If a correction in windage is necessary after the first shot is marked, it is determined as follows: The shot is plotted on the recording target of the score book; from the vertical center line through the bull's-eye the proper correction is noted and the aiming point for the following shot is shifted by this amount in the proper direction. The point of impact of the bullet will move in the same direction on the target as the aim is moved. For example, if it is desired to move the hits to the left, the aim must be moved to the left; if it is desired to make the hits strike to the right, the aim must be moved to the right.

b. *Elevation.*—Changing the elevation of the sight, or the aiming point at any range will cause a change in the location of the hit on the target. Changing the rear sight from the aperture set for 150 yards to that set for 300 will change the strike of the bullet on the target 20 inches for each hundred yards of range. For example: At 200 yards the first shot is fired with the 150 yard aperture. If the second shot is fired with the 300 yard aperture, the strike of the bullet will be 40 inches (approximate) higher than the strike of the first shot.

c. *Zero of a carbine.*—(1) The zero of a carbine for each range is the windage and elevation to be set on the rear sight, or the point on the target on which the sights of a carbine, without adjustable windage and elevation, must be alined in order to hit the center of the bull's-eye on a normal day when there is no wind. The zero of any carbine may differ with different men, owing to the difference in their hold or manner of aim.

(2) Each man must determine the zero of his own carbine for each range. He does this by studying the data which he has written in his score book concerning elevation of the rear sight, aiming points, changes in sight settings and aiming points, and the direction and velocity of the wind. The zero of a carbine is best found on a day when the sky is overcast and there is no wind. Having learned the zero of his carbine, the soldier computes all his windage and elevation allowances for the first shot from this zero, and the normal 6 o'clock aiming point.

d. *Shooting up or down hill.*—In shooting either up or down hill, less elevation is needed than when shooting on the level. The steeper the hill the less elevation is needed, so that when firing vertically up or down no elevation at all is needed, no matter how distant the target. Slight slopes that may be found on target ranges have no appreciable effect upon the elevation used and require no correction.

e. *Sight-setting and aiming point exercises using the* L *sight.*—In these exercises the instructor uses the full-sized A and B targets, with spotters to indicate the position of the hits.

(1) The instructor assembles his squad or group (each pupil having his carbine, score book, and pencil) and conducts the exercise as follows:

(a) Points out the two sight settings on the sight leaf.

(b) Explains the effect of wind and cautions the class to disregard all atmospheric influences except wind.

(c) Explains and demonstrates the methods of determining the amount of windage, that is, aiming point, for the first shot, and the corrections to make for subsequent shots.

(d) Tests the ability of the group to change sights or aiming point intelligently after the first shot by giving windage and elevation exercises.

(2) Examples of windage exercises are as follows:

(a) "You are at 200 yards and estimate the wind to be 10 miles from 9 o'clock. Plot your aiming point on the B recording target in your score book for the first shot. Evans, where has Little plotted his aiming point? Suppose you fired and the spotter marked the hit here (placing a spotter in the 4 space near the bull's-eye at 3 o'clock) and you were sure your hold and trigger squeeze were such that you have a perfect shot; plot your aiming point to bring the next shot in the vertical center line of the bull's-eye. Johnson, where has Williams plotted his aiming point? Each man whose teammate has not changed his aiming point to the left 12 inches, hold up his hand." The instructor assists those men who have decided errors by further explanation and illustration.

(b) The instructor gives a number of examples until the class thoroughly understands the methods of determining the amount of windage to take for the first shot and corrections, if necessary, in aiming points for subsequent shots.

(3) Following the instructions in taking windage, the in-

structor puts the class through similar exercises which require changes in elevation.

(4) Examples of elevation exercises are as follows:

(a) "You are at 200 yards, set your sights for 300 yards. There is no wind. Walsh, where is your aiming point for the first shot?" The instructor explains that since there is no wind the aim should be normal. "You fired and at the instant the shot went off you noticed that your sights were alined a little below and a little to the right of your zero aiming point. When the shot is marked you see that it struck a little to the right and 4 inches below (placing a spotter in the 4 space at 5 o'clock). You fired one more shot, and this time the aim was correct at the instant, that the rifle went off. This time the shot is marked here (placing a spotter about 4 inches in the 4 space just below the bottom edge of the bull's-eye). Allen, what are you going to do now? Lowe, what are you going to do? Both shots hit about the same distance below the bull's-eye, your trigger squeeze was perfect because you were able to call your shots close to where they actually hit, the variation in aim was very slight. Therefore you are justified in making a correction in your aiming point to raise the next shot to hit the center of the bull's-eye. Where will your new aiming point be?"

(b) The instructor then by explanations and illustrations assists those men who do not understand the procedure in arriving at the correct result.

(5) The instructor gives a number of examples which require changes in aiming point until the principles of aiming point changes are well understood.

(6) Examples of other sight-setting and aiming point exercises are as follows:

(a) "Set your sights at 300 yards, and place your aiming point on the 4 ring at 7 o'clock. Suppose you fire four shots hitting here (place four spotters in the bull's-eye), and your fifth shot here (place spotter on 3 space at 11 o'clock). Jones, what are you going to do now? Jenkins, what are you going to do? You should not do anything to the sight. It is practically certain that you squeezed the trigger improperly and flinched. Not even a sudden change in the weather could cause that much difference. Don't try to correct your own faults by changing the sights or aiming point."

(b) "For your first score in rapid fire at 200 yards you are using the same sight elevation that you used in zeroing the carbine on the rapid fire targets. Suppose this to be .50 yards elevation and your group goes here (putting 2 spotters low and to the left). What change in your aiming point would you make to bring the next score into the figure?"

(7) A group in rapid fire should strike the same place as in slow fire. Variation in the position of rapid-fire groups from slow-fire groups is due to imperfect trigger squeeze in rapid fire.

f. Use of the score book.—(1) Each man must keep a score book in which he records not only the value of the hits but the location of each hit, the sight setting and sight changes, the force and direction of the wind, the kind of light, the hour, the date, and such other data as may be of use in the future. Spaces for these notes are provided on the score sheets of the score book.

(2) The use of the score book on the range is important for the following reasons:

(a) The plotting of the shots shows the firer the location of his group and assists in determining the correct aiming point.

(b) Plotting the shots and recording the data as to light and wind help the soldier to learn the zero of his carbine.

(c) The data written down as to sight settings, aiming points and weather conditions while firing at any range are of great assistance in using the correct sight setting and determining the aiming point when again firing at that range. Where a number of scores have been fired and recorded, the firer should use the sight settings and aiming point from previous scores fired on days that were similar as to light and wind.

(3) The score book will be kept personally by the man firing. The coach assists him when necessary to decide what to write down, but the coach will neither plot the shots nor enter any data.

■ 53. Sixth Step—Examination of Men Before Starting Range Practice.—(The answers given herein are merely examples. Men should be required to explain them in their own words.)

Q. What is this (drawing a circle on the ground or holding up a cut-out circle)?—*A.* A circle.

Q. Where is the center of it?—*A.* Here (pointing to the center).

Q. What does this represent (showing an improvised enlarged front sight made of cardboard)?—*A.* The front sight of the carbine.

Q. Where should the top of the front sight be when it is correctly alined in the peep sight?—*A.* The top of the front sight should be in the center of the peep sight. (By use of the movable sights the instructor requires the pupil to adjust the front sight in proper alinement with the peep sight.)

Q. What is this (showing a movable bull's-eye)?—*A.* A bull's-eye.

Q. In aiming, is the bull's-eye in the center of the peep sight?—*A.* No; the bottom edge of it is in the center.

Q. Why?—*A.* Because the top of the front sight is in the center of the peep sight and just touches the bottom of the bull's-eye.

Q. Should the front sight be held up into the bottom of the bull's-eye?—*A.* No; it just touches the bottom edge of the bull's-eye, so that all of the bull's-eye can still be clearly seen.

Q. Why?—*A.* Because the front sight would blend with the bull's-eye and its position could not be accurately determined each time the aim is taken. Furthermore the top of the front sight would not be clearly defined and an error would result in centering the front sight in the peep. (The instructor requires the pupil to adjust the sights and bull's-eye to show the correct aim.)

Q. What is this (indicating sighting bar)?—*A.* Sighting bar.

Q. What is it for?—*A.* To teach me how to aim.

Q. Why is it better than a carbine for this purpose?—*A.* Because the sights on it are much larger and slight errors can be more easily seen and pointed out.

Q. What does this represent (indicating)?—*A.* The front sight.

Q. And this (indicating)?—*A.* The rear sight.

Q. What is this (indicating)?—*A.* The eyepiece.

Q. What is the eyepiece for?—A. To cause me to place my eye in such a position as to see the sights in the same alinement as that seen by the coach.

Q. Is there any eyepiece on the carbine?—A. No; I learn by the sighting bar how the sights look when properly alined, and I must hold my head so as to see the sights the same way when aiming a carbine.

Q. How do you hold your head steadily in this position when aiming a carbine?—A. By resting my cheek firmly against the side of the stock.

Q. Where do you focus your eye when aiming a carbine?—A. On the bull's-eye.

Q. What do you understand by the term "correct sight picture?"—A. It means that all the elements of the aim are in proper relationship to each other.

Q. Tell me what is wrong with these sight pictures. (The instructor now adjusts the sights of the bar, making various slight errors; first, to show the correct and incorrect adjustments of the sights, and then, with the sights properly adjusted, he sights on the small bull's-eye to demonstrate correct and incorrect adjustments, requiring the man to point out any errors.)

Q. Now, take this sighting bar and adjust the sights properly. (Verified by the instructor.)

Q. Now that the sights are properly adjusted, have the small bull's-eye moved until the sights are properly aimed at it.

Q. How do you breathe while aiming?—A. After I get my sights lined up on the bull's-eye, I draw in a little more than an ordinary breath, then let out a little and hold the remainder while.aiming and squeezing the trigger.

Q. Take the prone position, aim and simulate firing a shot at that mark. (The instructor must assure himself that the man knows how to hold his breath properly while aiming. Many men have great difficulty in learning to do this correctly.)

Q. I will take the carbine and assume the kneeling, sitting, and prone positions, and you will tell me whether the position is correct or incorrect in each case.

Q. Now show me how you take the sitting and prone positions rapidly from a standing position.

Q. How do you squeeze the trigger?—*A.* By pressing the trigger straight to the rear so steadily and smoothly that I do not know when the rifle will go off.

Q. What do you check and concentrate on while you are squeezing the trigger?—*A.* On the sight picture to see that it is correct.

Q. If the sights are out of alinement with the aiming point, what do you do?—*A.* I hold the pressure I have on the trigger and only resume the increase of pressure when the sights become lined upon the aiming point again.

Q. If you do this, can your shot be a bad one?—*A.* No.

Q. Why?—*A.* Because I cannot flinch, for I do not know when to flinch; and the sights will always be lined up with the aiming point when the rifle goes off, because I never increase the pressure on the trigger, except when they are properly lined up.

Q. Is it necessary to take a long time to press the trigger in this way?—*A.* No. The method of squeezing the trigger is slow at first, but rapidity is developed by practice.

Q. How do you squeeze the trigger in rapid fire?—*A.* I squeeze it the same way as in slow fire, with a steady continuous increase of pressure so I do not know when the rifle will fire.

Q. In rapid fire how do you gain time so as not to be compelled to hurry in aiming and squeezing the trigger?—*A.* I gain time by taking the position rapidly, by counting the shots of the first magazine, by quick reloading, and by keeping my eye on the target.

Q. Is it important to get into the correct position before beginning to shoot in rapid fire?—*A.* Yes; even though it takes more time, I should always get into the correct position before beginning to shoot.

Q. What is meant by calling the shot?—*A.* To say where you think the bullet hit as soon as you shoot and before the shot is marked.

Q. How can you do this?—*A.* By noticing exactly where the sights point when the rifle goes off.

Q. If a man cannot call his shot properly, what does it usually indicate?—*A.* That he did not squeeze the trigger properly and did not know where the sights pointed at the time the carbine went off.

Q. What is this (showing a score book)?—*A.* A score book.

Q. If a shot hits here (indicating), what change in your sight or aiming point would you make to bring the next shot to the center of the bull's-eye?

Q. What effect does changing the setting of your rear sight or your aiming point have on the shot?—*A.* It moves it in the same direction as the change in setting of the rear sight or aiming point is moved.

Q. If you want to make a shot hit higher, what do you do?—*A.* I increase my elevation or raise my aiming point.

Q. If you want to make your shots hit more to the right, what do you do?—*A.* I move my aiming point to the right.

Q. How do you determine the amount of windage to take for the first shot?—*A.* By estimating the velocity and direction of the wind, then by using the windage rule I get approximately the number of inches to change my aiming point.

Q. Give me an example.

Q. How do you determine the direction of the wind?—*A.* I face the target and consider myself as occupying the center of the dial of a horizontal clock. I then note the direction of the wind in reference to the numbers on the dial.

Q. I will place this spotter on this target (full size 300-yard target) to represent a shot properly fired by you at 300 yards with sight set at 300 yards. What change would you make in your aiming point for your next shot? (Instructor now tests in various ways the man's ability to make proper aiming point corrections.)

Q. What are the three principal uses of the score book?—*A.* To show me where my shot group is located, to indicate how much change in windage and elevation (aiming point) is necessary to move a shot or group of shots to the center of the target, and to make a record of the sight settings and aiming point of my carbine for the different ranges under various weather conditions so that I will know how to set my sight and where to aim when starting to shoot at each range under different weather conditions.

Q. Tell me what effect different light and weather conditions have on a man's shooting.

Q. In firing at ranges up to and including 300 yards, what is the only weather condition for which you make corrections?—*A.* Wind.

69

Q. What three things do you do in cleaning a carbine after it has been fired?—A. I first remove the powder fouling from the bore. I then dry the bore thoroughly. After this is done I swab the bore thoroughly with light rust-preventive compound to protect it from rust.

Q. How do you remove the powder fouling from the bore?—A. By swabbing it thoroughly with cleaning patches saturated with warm water or warm, soapy water.

Q. How do you dry the bore?—A. By running clean patches through the bore until it is thoroughly dry.

Q. How do you protect the bore from rust?—A. By swabbing it thoroughly with a cleaning patch saturated with light rust-preventive compound or light preservative lubricating oil issued for this purpose.

SECTION III

QUALIFICATION COURSES

■ 54. GENERAL.—See AR 775–10 for information as to who will fire the course, individual classification, qualification, ammunition allowances, etc.

■ 55. INSTRUCTION PRACTICE.—The following tables prescribe the firing of instruction practice in the order followed by the individual soldier.

TABLE I.—*Slow fire* [1]

Range	Time	Shots	Target	Position	Remarks
100	No limit_____	10	A	Prone_____	W/sling.
200	___:_do_____	10	B	_____do_____	Do.
300	_____do_____	10	B	_____do_____	Do.

[1] To be fired only by men who have never previously qualified in a course in rifle or carbine marksmanship.

TABLE II.—*Slow fire* [1]

Range	Time	Shots	Target	Position	Remarks
100	1 min. per shot_____	4	A	Sitting_____	W/o sling.
100	_____do_____	4	A	Kneeling____	Do.
100	_____do_____	4	A	Standing____	Do.
200	_____do_____	4	B	Sitting_____	Do.
200	_____do_____	4	B	Kneeling____	Do.
200	_____do_____	5	B	Standing____	Do.
300	_____do_____	5	B	Prone_____	Do.

[1] Men who have previously qualified in a course of rifle or carbine marksmanship will fire table II only once for practice. Men who have never previously qualified in a course of rifle or carbine marksmanship will fire table II twice for practice.

TABLE III.—*Rapid fire*[1]

Range	Time (seconds)	Shots	Target	Position	Remarks
100	35	8 (2 mags., 4 each)	2 A centers on a 6 x 6 frame (see fig. 25).	Standing (1 mag., 4 rds.); sitting (1 mag., 4 rds.).	Fire 4 rounds standing at *top A center*; reload, take sitting position, and fire 4 rounds at *bottom A center.*
100	35	8 (2 mags., 4 each)	2 A centers on a 6 x 6 frame (see fig. 25).	Standing (1 mag., 4 rds.); kneeling (1 mag., 4 rds.).	Fire 4 rounds standing at *top A center*; reload, take kneeling position, and fire 4 rounds at *bottom A center.*
200	35	8 (2 mags., 4 each)	2 B centers on a 6 x 6 frame (see fig. 25).	Standing (1 mag., 4 rds.); sitting (1 mag., 4 rds.).	Fire 4 rounds standing at *top B center*; reload, take sitting position, and fire 4 rounds at *bottom B center.*
200	35	8 (2 mags., 4 each)	2 B centers on a 6 x 6 frame (see fig. 25).	Standing (1 mag., 4 rds.); kneeling (1 mag., 4 rds.).	Fire 4 rounds standing at *top B center*; reload, take kneeling position, and fire 4 rounds at *bottom B center.*
300	35	8 (2 mags., 4 each)	1 B center on a 6 x 6 frame (see fig. 25).	Standing to prone	Take prone position, fire 4 rounds at *B center*; reload, fire 4 more rounds.

[1] Men who have previously qualified in a course of rifle or carbine marksmanship will fire table III only once for practice. Men who have never previously qualified in a course of rifle or carbine marksmanship will fire table III twice for practice.

71

■ **56. Record Practice.**—Table III of instruction practice is fired once for record.

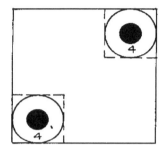

100 Yards
(2 A centers)

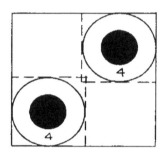

200 Yards
(2 B centers)

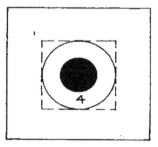

300 Yards
(1 B center)

Figure 25.—Arrangement of target centers for rapid fire.

Section IV

RANGE PRACTICE

■ **57. General.**—*a. Phases.*—Range practice is started immediately after completion of the preparatory training.

Range practice is divided into two parts—instruction practice and record practice.

b. *Sequence.*—Each person will complete instruction practice before he proceeds with record practice. Instruction practice and record practice will not be conducted simultaneously except on ranges where the firing points are in echelon or where the two types of practice are conducted on different parts of the same range.

c. *Range personnel.*—(1) *Officer in charge of firing.*—An officer in charge of firing will be designated by the responsible commander. It is desirable that he be the senior officer of the largest organization occupying the range. The officer in charge of firing, or his deputy, will be present during all firing and will be in charge of the firing and safety precautions on the range.

(2) *Range officer.*—The range officer is appointed by the post commander and is responsible to him for maintaining and assigning ranges, designating danger zones, and closing roads leading into danger zones. The range officer makes timely arrangements for material and labor to place the ranges in proper condition for range practice. He directs and supervises all necessary repairs to shelters, butts, targets, firing points, and telephone lines. He provides for the safety of the markers, and when necessary he provides range guards and instructs them in the methods to be used for the protection of life and property within the danger area. He assists the officer in charge of firing by using the means necessary to provide efficient service from the maintenance personnel of the ranges.

(3) *Range noncommissioned officer.*—A noncommissioned officer and such assistants as the post commander may deem necessary will be detailed permanently during the range practice season as assistant to the range officer. He is responsible to the range officer that the target and pit equipment is kept in serviceable condition; that the desired targets are ready for use at the appointed time; and that all targets and pit details are provided with the proper flags, marking disks, pasters, and spotters.

(4) *Pit details.*—Commanders of organizations firing will provide such detail of officers, noncommissioned officers, and

privates as may be necessary to supervise, operate, mark, and score the targets used by their respective organizations.

d. Uniform.—The uniform to be worn during instruction practice and record practice will be prescribed by the commanding officer.

e. Pistol belt.—The pistol belt with magazine pouch will be worn during instruction practice and record firing.

f. Safety precautions.—(1) Safety precautions for troops are complete in this manual. Reference to AR 750–10 is necessary for range officers, the officer in charge of firing, and the commander responsible for the location of ranges and the conduct of firing. All officers and men who are to fire or who are concerned with range practice will be familiarized with the safety precautions before firing is commenced.

(2) Danger flags will be displayed at prominent positions on the range during firing. There will be no firing until these flags are displayed.

(3) The carbines of an organization will be inspected upon their arrival at the range by the officers to see that chambers and barrels are free from obstruction and that all bolts are open.

(4) Consider every carbine to be loaded until it is examined and found to be unloaded. Never trust your memory as to its condition in this respect.

(5) When the bolt is closed, never point the carbine in any direction where an accidental discharge may cause harm.

(6) Firing will not begin on any range until the officer in charge of firing has determined that the range is clear and has given the commands LOAD and COMMENCE FIRING.

(7) At least one officer will be present at all firing.

(8) All carbines on the range except those in use on the firing line and those in use during supervised preparatory training will be *clear*, with bolts *open* at all times.

(9) No carbine will be removed from the firing line until an officer or specially selected noncommissioned officer has inspected it to see that it is clear and the bolt open.

(10) No person will be allowed in front of the firing line for any purpose until directed by an officer who has ordered all carbines to be cleared and determined that the order has been carried out.

(11) All firing will immediately cease and carbines be cleared at the command: CEASE FIRING.

(12) Cartridges will not be left chambered in hot barrels.

(13) All loading and unloading will be executed on the firing line with the muzzles directed toward the targets. Carbines will never be loaded in rear of the firing line.

(14) Care will be taken to avoid undue exposure of ammunition to the direct rays of the sun. This creates hazardous chamber pressures.

(15) Never grease or oil the ammunition or walls of the carbine chamber.

(16) See that the ammunition is clean and dry. Examine all ammunition and turn in all with loose bullets or which appear to be otherwise defective.

(17) Never fire a carbine with any rust-preventive compound, cleaning patch, dust, dirt, sand, snow, or other obstruction in the bore. To do so may burst the barrel.

(18) Before leaving the range, all carbines and magazine pouches will be inspected by an officer to see that they do not contain ammunition. Men in ranks will be directed to search their clothing to be sure that they have no ammunition in their possession.

(19) See AR 45–30 for regulations covering report of accident involving ordnance matériel.

■ 58. INSTRUCTION PRACTICE.—*a. General.*—Instruction practice represents the application with service ammunition of the principles taught in the preparatory training. The instruction practice outlined for the course is designed to serve as a guide only. Within authorized ammunition allowances the number of shots to be fired at each range is discretionary with the organization commander. The amount of instruction practice is not limited to that outlined in the tables. Such additional practice as time and ammunition allowances permit should be given.

b. Organization of firing line.—(1) *General.*—The firing line will be organized so as to insure safe and orderly conduct, to provide maximum training and instruction, so that all men will be kept busy all the time, and to facilitate supervision by the officer in charge of firing, and his assistants.

(2) *Procedure.*—(*a*) Two teams, each consisting of a pupil

and his coach, are assigned tó a target. One team works on the right and the other team on the left of the stake indicating the number of the target, or pair of targets on the firing point. The pupil on the right, assisted by his coach fires his instruction practice first. During this firing the pupil of the team on the left "dry shoots." When the firer of the right team completeš his instruction practice, the "dry shooter" of the team on the left fires his instruction practice from the same position he used while "dry shooting." During this firing the team on the right exchange places, i. e., the coach becomes the pupil and the pupil the coach, and the pupil "dry shoots." The teams, and the individuals within the teams thus alternate firing, dry shooting, and coaching until all men of both teams have completed their practice firing.

(b) If sufficient space is not available to provide room on the firing line for two teams per target or pair of targets, remaining teams are given "dry shooting" practice on the flanks or at a point not less than 50 yards in rear of the firing line while awaiting their turn to fire. Safety precautions will be strictly enforced during such practice.

(3) *Rest periods.*—No men are permitted to fall out of their training assignment, except at the 10-minute rest period given at the end of each hour. The beginning and termination of this period is indicated by the officer in charge of instruction.

(4) *Slow and rapid fire.*—The above organization and procedure is applicable to both slow and rapid fire.

c. *Slow fire.*—The first few shots fired on the range by beginners will be slow fire from the prone position to facilitate instruction in the proper method of squeezing the trigger. The prone position assures such a steady hold that the temptation of the beginner to snap in his shot at the instant the sight touches the bull's-eye is eliminated. This fault is the cause of nearly all poor shooting. In the prone position the sights can be held close to the bottom of the bull's-eye while the firer squeezes the trigger with such a smooth, steady pressure as not to know exactly when the carbine will fire. This is the basis of all good shooting. The habit of squeezing the trigger correctly, acquired by firing from the prone position, will in all probability be retained while firing in the more unsteady positions—sitting, kneeling, and standing.

d. *Rapid fire.*—During rapid fire the tendency to jerk the trigger, and consequently to flinch, is very marked. This tendency must be corrected before it becomes a fixed habit.

e. *Coaching.*—(1) *General.*—The firer works under the supervision of a coach. This does not mean that each man must have an experienced shot beside him. Any man of intelligence who has been properly instructed in the preparatory work and who has been given instruction in coaching methods can be used with good results and should be used

FIGURE 26.—Position of coach.

when more experienced shots are not available. It is good practice to have expert coaches in charge of one or more targets, usually on a flank, to which particularly difficult pupils are sent for special coaching. Great patience should be exercised by the coach so as not to excite or confuse the firer.

(2) *Position of coach* (fig. 26).—On the firing line, the coach will take a position similar to that of the man who is firing—prone, sitting, kneeling, or standing—so as to be able to watch his trigger finger and his eye. In the later stages of instruction firing, the coach may be withdrawn from the firing line to observe his pupil from a point in rear; this affords the coach an opportunity to observe the pupil's per-

formance while he is working alone, as he will be in record practice. The pupil's errors should be noted and brought to his attention at the completion of the score.

(3) *Watching the eye.*—Errors in trigger squeeze, which are the most serious and the hardest to correct, can be detected by watching the pupil's eye. If his eye closes as the carbine goes off, he knew when it was going off and therefore did not squeeze the trigger properly. The explosion and the shock cause a man to wink, but this wink cannot be seen, because of the sudden movement of the head that takes place at the same time. If the firer can be seen to wink it is because he winked first and jerked the trigger afterward.

(4) *Preventing flinching.*—The best method of curing flinching is to prevent it. One of the most important duties of the coach is to detect indications that his pupil is about to flinch. Inclination to flinch can be detected by watching the pupil's head and eye while he is squeezing the trigger. If, during the application of squeeze to the trigger, the pupil's eye begins to twitch and his head is gradually drawn away from the thumb or stock it is a sure sign he will flinch. As soon as the coach notices these conditions he should require the pupil to bring the carbine down from the firing position, rest a few seconds and start all over again. While the pupil is resting, the coach points out his errors, such as not taking up the slack, applying the squeeze with a series of impulses instead of continuous pressure, and concentrating on the discharge instead of on the sight picture. If the pupil is seen to be flinching the coach has him turn his head aside while he, the coach, puts in a cartridge and shoves the bolt home. The coach frequently simulates loading without letting the pupil know what he has done. Thus the flinch, indicated by the shoulder being shoved forward at the same time that the trigger is pressed, will be evident even to the firer himself. The coach then proves to him by squeezing the trigger a few times (as explained in (5) below) that his poor shooting is due to faulty trigger squeeze.

(5) *Coach squeezing trigger.*—(a) To squeeze the trigger for the firer, the coach lies with his right elbow on the ground to steady his hand, places his thumb against the trigger, and his first finger against the back of the trigger

guard. In this way he can apply pressure to the trigger by a pinching action of his thumb and first finger (see fig. 27).

(*b*) The coach then watches the firer's back, and between 5 and 10 seconds after the firer begins to hold his breath, he applies enough pressure to discharge the piece. Shots fired in this way are almost always accurately placed. After firing the piece a few times the coach lets the firer try a

FIGURE 27.—Coach squeezing trigger.

few shots alone to see if he can squeeze the trigger the same way the coach squeezed it, so as not to know just when the piece will go off. Sometimes it is necessary to repeat this exercise, but the majority of beginners can be permanently cured of the tendency to flinch by a few minutes of this kind of coaching. Old shots who are flinchers require more time and patience.

(6) *Duties of coach in slow fire.*—The coach observes the pupil carefully and corrects all errors. He pays particular attention to see—

(*a*) That the sights are blackened and that they are set at the correct range.

(b) That the ammunition is free from dirt.

(c) That the pupil has the correct position, body at the proper angle, elbows correctly placed, and the cheek pressed firmly against the stock.

(d) That the pupil is holding his breath properly (by watching his back occasionally).

(e) That the slack is taken up promptly.

(f) That the trigger squeeze is continued from that point with a smooth, steady, continuous increase.

(g) Whether or not the pupil flinches (by watching his eye, the head or the front sight for flips).

(h) That the pupil calls his shot each time he fires.

(i). That the pupil keeps his score book correctly.

(7) *Duties of coach in rapid fire.*—(a) The coach observes the pupil carefully and corrects all errors. He pays particular attention to see—

1. That the sights are blackened and that they are set at the proper range.

2. That the pupil assumes the correct position before he starts firing.

3. That he takes up the slack promptly.

4. That he presses the trigger continuously until the shot is fired.

5. Whether or not the pupil flinches (by watching his eye).

6. That he changes position promptly.

7. That he reloads deliberately and accurately.

8. That he fires the required number of shots at each target center.

(b) These operations follow each other, and the coach can watch each in turn. The coach will also at times watch the pupil's back to see if he holds his breath while firing each shot.

(c) Any lack of smooth and proper timing in firing indicates that the preparatory training has not be sufficient, and additional preparatory rapid-fire practice will be given.

f. *Individual precautions.*—(1) *Slow fire.*—The pupil should take the following precautions during every slow-fire score:

(*a*) Be sure that both the front and rear sights of the carbine are properly blackened.

(*b*) Be sure that the rear sight is properly set for the first shot.

(*c*) Take the score book with preliminary data properly filled in, to the firing point.

(*d*) Fire the first shot very carefully and then, if necessary, change the sights (or the aiming point) to bring the second shot into the bull's-eye.

(*e*) Plot each shot in the score book.

(*f*) Before changing the sight setting, or the aiming point, note the setting on the sights and determine the amount of change required from a study of the shots plotted in the score book. Record the corrected sight setting and the aiming point.

(*g*) Do not change the sights or the aiming point unnecessarily. If a bad shot is made closely following several good shots it is almost certain to be the fault of the firer.

(2) *Rapid fire.*—In rapid-fire practice the pupil should be sure that his sights are blackened and properly set. Upon completion of a score he should carefully plot each shot in the score book and promptly record any changes in the aiming point that may be necessary to center the group in the bull's-eye.

g. *Use of instruments.*—The use of binoculars, telescopes, sight-setting instruments, and instruments or devices for determining the force and direction of the wind is authorized and encouraged during instruction practice.

h. Procedure prescribed in paragraph 59 for record practice is applicable to instruction practice with the following exceptions:

(1) Scores are not required to be kept in the pits.

(2) Only such officers and noncommissioned officers are on duty in the pits as are necessary to preserve order and insure efficient pit service.

(3) The manner in which the scores are kept on the firing line is discretionary with the organization commander.

■ 59. RECORD PRACTICE.—*a. General.*—(1) The purpose of record practice is to test the soldier's skill with the carbine and to determine his qualification. The qualification course is prescribed in section III.

(2) The sequence in which the scores are fired in record practice is discretionary with the officer in charge of firing.

(3) Whenever practicable during record practice the officers required for duty in the pits will be detailed from troops not firing.

b. *Organization of firing line.*—(1) *General.*—The firing line will be organized to insure safe and orderly conduct and to facilitate supervision of the firing by the officer in charge of firing and his assistants. The distances specified in (2) below should be used as a guide only and may be modified at the discretion of the officer in charge of firing to meet local conditions.

(2) *Establishments.*—(a) Scorers stationed in rear of the firing line and close to the soldier being scored.

(b) Ammunition line 5 yards in rear of the firing line.

(c) Telephone operators 5 yards in rear of the ammunition line.

(d) Soldiers awaiting their turn to fire (*ready line*), 5 yards in rear of the line of telephone operators.

(e) Carbine rests and cleaning racks 10 yards in rear of the ready line.

(3) *Firing assignments.*—Individuals who are to fire will be assigned targets and the order in which they will take turn in firing the several scores, that is, first order, second order, etc.

c. *Pit details.*—The details for the supervision, operation, marking, and scoring of targets during record practice consist of—

(1) One commissioned officer assigned to each two targets. When it is impracticable to detail one officer to each two targets, an officer will be assigned to supervise the marking and scoring of not to exceed four targets. In this event the pit scores will be kept by the noncommissioned officer in charge of each target, who will sign the score card.

(2) One noncommissioned officer assigned to each target, or set of two targets, to direct and supervise the markers. This noncommissioned officer will be selected from a company or organization other than the one firing on the target which

he supervises.   If this is not possible the officer assigned to the target will exercise special care to insure correct scoring.

(3) One or two privates assigned to operate and mark each target. These privates may be selected from the organization firing on the target to which they are assigned.

d. Score cards and scoring.—(1) Two score cards will be kept, one at the firing point and one in the pit.

(2) Entries on all score cards will be made in ink or with indelible pencil.   No alteration or correction will be made on the card except by the organization commander, who will initial each alteration or correction made.

(3) The cards at the firing point will bear the date, the firer's name, the number of the target and the order of firing. The pit card will not show the firer's name but will bear the date, the number of the target, and the order of firing.

(4) The scores at each firing point will be kept by a noncommissioned officer of some organization other than that firing on the target to which he is assigned.   If this is not possible company officers will exercise special care to insure correct scoring.   As soon as a score is completed the score card will be signed by the scorer, taken up, signed by the officer supervising the scoring, and turned over to the organization commander.   Except when required for entering new scores on the range, score cards will be retained in the personal possession of the organization commander.

(5) In the pit the officer keeps the scores for the targets to which he is assigned.   As soon as a score is completed he signs the score card.   He turns these cards over to the organization commander at the end of the day's firing.   The organization commander will check the pit records against the firing line records.   In case of discrepancy between the two records the provisions of AR 345–1000 will apply.

(6) Upon completion of record firing and after the qualification order is issued, the pit score cards of each man will be attached to his official score card kept at the firing point. For records and reports of qualification see AR 345–1000.

e. Marking.—(1) The value of the shot is indicated as follows:

(*a*) A bull's-eye, or five, with a white disk.

(*b*) A four with a red disk.

(c) All other shots are spotted but marked as misses by waving a red flag across the front of the target, once for each shot.

(2) Spotters are placed in the shot holes before the target is run up for marking.

(3) The marking begins with the hits of highest value, the center of the disk being placed over the spotter, then swung off the target and back again to the next spotter, care being taken each time to show only the face of the disk indicating the value of the shot being marked. The marking will be slow enough to avoid confusing the scorer at the firing point. When one spotter covers more than one shot hole the disk is placed over it the required number of times.

f. Procedure.—(1) *On firing line.*—(a) One person will be assigned to a target in each order (see fig. 25).

(b) When all is ready in the pit a red flag is displayed at the center target. At that signal the officer in charge of the firing line commands: LOAD. The carbines are loaded and locked.

(c) The officer in charge of the firing line then calls so that all may hear, "Ready on the right?" "Ready on the left?" Anyone who is not ready calls out, "Not ready on No. —."

(d) All being ready on the firing line, the officer in charge commands: READY ON THE FIRING LINE. Carbines are unlocked and the position of READY assumed. The telephone orderly notifies the pit, "Ready on the firing line."

(e) The flag at the center target is waved and then withdrawn. Five seconds after the flag is withdrawn the targets appear, remain fully exposed for the prescribed period of time, and are then withdrawn. The firer takes the prescribed position as soon as the targets appear and commences firing. At 100 and 200 yards he fires or attempts to fire four shots at the upper target center, changes position, if required, reloading from a magazine containing four rounds taken from the magazine pouch, fires or attempts to fire four rounds at the lower target center. At 300 yards he fires two magazines of four rounds each from the same position at one target center. If any individual fails to fire at all he will be given another opportunity.

(*f*) As soon as the targets are withdrawn the officer in charge commands: UNLOAD. All unfired cartridges are removed from the carbines, and the bolts are left open. The men remain in position on the firing line until they are ordered off by the officer in charge.

(*g*) As each shot is signaled it is announced as follows: "Target No. —, 1 five, 2 fives, 3 fives, 1 four, 2 fours, 3 fours, 1 miss." The scorer notes these values on a pad and watches the target as he calls the shot. After the marking is finished he counts the number of shots marked, and if more or less than 8 calls "Re-mark No. —." If 8 shots have been marked he then enters the score on the soldier's score card and totals it as follows: 5 5 5 4 4 4 0 0 equals 27.

(2) *In pit.*—(*a*) The time is regulated in the pit by the officer in charge.

(*b*) When all is ready in the pit the targets are fully withdrawn and a red flag is displayed at the center target.

(*c*) When the message is received that the firing line is ready, the red flag at the center target is waved and withdrawn and the command: READY is given to the pit details.

(*d*) Five seconds after the red flag is withdrawn the targets, by command or signal, are run up, left fully exposed for the prescribed period of time, and then withdrawn.

(*e*) The officers in the pit examine each of their targets in turn, announce the score, and record it on the pit score card. Spotters are then placed in the shot holes, and the targets run up and marked. The noncommissioned officer supervises the marking of each shot. The officer exercises general supervision over the marking.

(*f*) The targets are left up for about 1 minute after being marked and are then withdrawn, pasted, and made ready for another score. They may be left up until ordered pasted by the officer in charge of the firing line.

g. Use of telephones.—(1) Telephones will be used for official communication only.

(2) No one will ask over the telephone for information as to the name or organization of any person firing on any

particular target, and no information of this nature will be transmitted.

(3) The following expressions will be used over the telephone in the situations indicated:

(a) When a shot has been fired and the target has not been withdrawn from the firing position, "Mark No. ——."

(b) When a shot has been fired and the target withdrawn from the firing position but not marked, "Disk No. ——."

(c) When the target has been withdrawn from the firing position and marked, but the value of the shot has not been understood, "Re-disk No. ——."

(d) When the firing line is ready for rapid fire, "Ready on the firing line."

(e) When a shot is marked on a target and the person assigned thereto has not fired, "Disregard the last shot on No. ——."

h. *Miscellaneous rules governing record practice.*—(1) *Identity of firer to be unknown to personnel in pit.*—Officers and men in the pit should not know who is firing on any particular target.

(2) *Trigger pull.*—The trigger pull will be at least 3 pounds and before record firing will be tested (with the barrel vertical) by an officer.

(3) *Ammunition.*—The ammunition used will be the U. S. carbine cartridge, caliber .30, M1, as issued by the Ordnance Department, unless the use of other ammunition is authorized.

(4) *Cleaning.*—Cleaning will be permitted only between scores.

(5) *Pads.*—Pads of moderate size and thickness may be worn on both elbows. Shoulder pads will not be worn.

(6) *Sling.*—The sling will not be used.

(7) *Loading pieces.*—Pieces will not be loaded except by command or until position for firing has been taken.

(8) *Warming or fouling shots.*—No warming or fouling shots will be allowed.

(9) *Coaching.*—Firers may be coached during record practice except when additional compensation for qualification is authorized.

(10) *Action in case of disabled carbine.*—Should a breakage occur the carbine will be repaired or a different carbine

substituted. If a different carbine is substituted the firer will be allowed to zero the sustituted carbine and then re-fire the exercise.

(11) *Shots cutting the edge of bull's-eye or line.*—Any shot cutting the edge of the figure or bull's-eye will be signaled and recorded as a hit in the figure or the bull's-eye. Because the limiting line of each division of the target is the outer edge of the line separating it from the exterior division, a shot touching this line will be signaled and recorded as a hit in the higher division.

(12) *Misses.*—In all firing, before any miss is signaled, the target will be withdrawn from the firing position and carefully examined by an officer, if an officer is on duty in the pit. Whenever the target is run up and a miss is signaled, it will be presumed that this examination has been thoroughly made. No challenge of the value signaled will be entertained or resignaling of the shot allowed.

(13) *Accidental discharges.*—All shots fired by the soldier after he has taken his place at the firing point (and it is his turn to fire, the target being ready) will be considered in his score even if his piece was not directed toward the target or was accidentally discharged.

(14) *Firing on wrong target.*—Shots fired upon the wrong target will be entered as a miss upon the score of the man firing, no matter what the value of the hit upon the wrong target may be. The soldier at fault is credited with only such shots as he may have made on his own target.

(15) *Misfires.*—In event of a misfire the soldier will cease firing immediately, the target will not be marked, and the score will be repeated.

(16) *Unfired cartridges.*—Each unfired cartridge will be recorded as a miss. If the number of hits marked exceeds the number of rounds fired, the soldier firing on that target will be credited with the hits of highest value corresponding to the number of rounds fired.

(17) *Disabled carbine.*—If during the firing of a score the carbine becomes disabled through no fault of the soldier, the pit officer will be directed to disregard the score, the target will not be marked, and the firer will repeat the score.

(18) *More than 8 hits.*—When a pair of targets (or the

single target at 300 yards) has more than 8 hits, the score will not be marked, and the soldier will fire again; except when all the hits have the same value, the score will be marked, and the firer will be given that value for each shot fired by him.

Section V

EQUIPMENT—KNOWN-DISTANCE TARGETS AND RANGES

■ 60. Equipment.—*a. Equipment for preparatory marksmanship training.*—(1) *General.*—The use during preparatory marksmanship training of complicated apparatus which cannot be readily improvised from materials at hand is unnecessary. The simple apparatus described below is ample for all purposes.

(2) *Equipment for each four men.*
   1 sighting bar, complete.
   1 large peep sight, 1 large front sight, and 1 large bull's-eye (all made of cardboard)
   1 carbine rest.
   1 small sighting disk.
   2 small aiming targets (target A and B, rifle, 1,000-inch range are suitable)
   1 10-inch sighting disk.
   1 small box, approximately the size of an ammunition box.
   1 frame covered with blank paper for long-range triangles.
   2 sandbags.
   1 pencil.
   4 score books (1 per man).
   1 form showing state of training for each squad.
   Material for blackening sights.
(3) *Equipment for general use.*
   1 double bull's-eye target with curtain for each three squads.
   1 A and 1 B target on frames for score-book exercises.
   Cleaning and preserving materials.

(4) *Preparation of equipment.*—(a) *Sighting bar.*

    1. Provide a bar of wood about 1 by 2 inches and 4½ feet long. Cut two thin slots 1 inch deep across the edge. Place one slot 5½ inches from the end and the other 26 inches from the same end of the bar (fig. 28② and ③).

    2. Make a front sight ½ inch wide, of thin metal 1½ by 3 inches, with wing guards ⅛ inch wide extending ¼ inch on both sides of front sight and ¼ inch above height of the front sight. Bend in the shape of an L and tack it to the edge of the bar between the two slots and ½ inch from the slot nearest the end (fig. 28① and ④). Have the leg of the L project above bar ½ to ¾ inch (fig. 28①).

    3. Make an eyepiece from a piece of tin or zinc 3 by 7 inches (fig. 28④). Cut along the dotted lines to form a shape shown in figure. Tack this eyepiece to the end of the bar farthest from the slots so that the top of the eyepiece extends 1 inch above the top of the bar (fig. 28①). Make a round hole 0.03 inch in diameter in the middle of the eyepiece ½ inch above the bar.

    4. Make a peep rear sight of thin metal or cardboard 3 by 3 inches and cut a round hole ¾ inch in diameter in its center (fig. 28④).

    5. Cut an open rear sight of thin metal or cardboard 1½ by 3 inches width a semicircular notch ¾ inch wide in the middle of one of the long edges (fig. 28④).

    6. Cut a piece of thin metal or cardboard 3 by 3 inches, painted white, and have a black bull's-eye ½ inch in diameter painted or pasted on the center (fig. 28④).

    7. Place two pieces of tin 1 inch wide and 3 inches long in each slot. Fold the loose ends away from each other and tack them to the sides of the bar (fig. 28③).

8. Blacken the eyepiece, the front sight, the rear
sights and the top of the bar.

(*b*) *Carbine rest.*—An empty ammunition box or any other
well-made box of suitable size, with notches cut in the ends

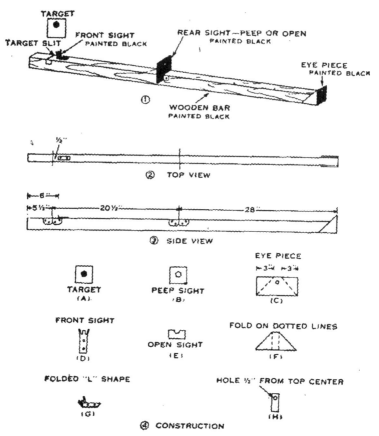

FIGURE 28.—Construction of sighting bar.

to fit the carbine closely, makes a good rest. The carbine is
placed in these notches with the trigger guard close to and
outside of one end. The sling is loosened and pulled to one
side. The box may be half filled with earth or sand to give
it greater stability.

(*c*) *Sighting disks.*—Sighting disks are of two sizes. The
disk to be used at a distance of 50 feet is about 3 inches in

90

diameter. The disk is made of tin or cardboard and mounted on a handle as shown in figure 29. The bull's-eye will be mounted on a background of clean, white paper. The disks to be used at 100 and 200 yards are 10 inches in diameter. These disks are painted black and mounted on white handles which are 4 or 5 feet long. All bull's-eyes will be black and circular and will have a hole in the center large enough to admit the point of a pencil.

    b. *Range equipment.*—(1) *Used at firing point.*

        Cleaning racks.
        Scorers' tables.
        Field glasses (1 per target).
        Score cards.
        Score board.
        Cleaning and preserving materials.
        Material for blackening sights.
        Score books.
        Indelible pencils.
        Containers for empty cartridge cases.
        Telephones.

    (2) *Used in pit.*

        Pit record cards.
        Indelible pencils.
        Telephones.
        Eight 3-inch spotters per target.
        Eight 6-inch spotters per target.
        One red flag per target.
        Marking disks.
        Pasters.
        Paste.

■ 61. Targets.—*a.* The A target center is used for 100 yards. It is a square 27 inches on a side. It contains a 10-inch black, circular bull's-eye and one ring 26 inches in diameter. A hit in the bull's-eye has a value of five. A hit outside the bull's-eye but within the 26-inch ring has a value of four. Hits outside the 26-inch ring have no value.

    b. The B target center is used for 200 and 300 yards. It is a square 38 inches on a side. It contains a 20-inch black, circular bull's-eye and one ring 37 inches in diameter. The values of hits are the same as on the A target center.

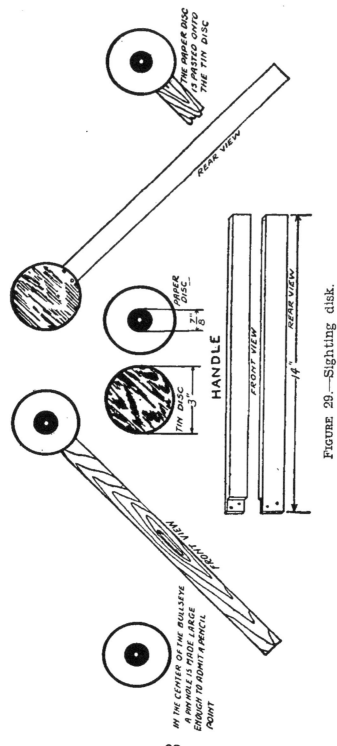

FIGURE 29.—Sighting disk.

CHAPTER 3

MARKSMANSHIP—MOVING GROUND TARGETS

SECTION I

GENERAL

■ 62. EMPLOYMENT.—Personnel armed with the carbine will be trained to fire at moving ground targets, such as personnel, trucks, and reconnaissance vehicles at appropriate ranges. (For air targets sec. ch. 4.) Fire directed at the vision slits and periscopes of moving tanks may blind the occupants. Personnel armed with the carbine will be trained to use their weapons against these targets.

■ 63. FUNDAMENTALS.—The fundamentals of shooting at moving targets are presented in this chapter. In applying these fundamentals the firer must adjust his aim and trigger squeeze to conform to the movement of the target.

, a. *Effective range*.—Under ideal conditions moving targets may be engaged with the carbine at ranges up to 300 yards. For this reason training in the technique of fire is limited to ranges up to 300 yards.

b. *Sights*.—Moving targets are seldom exposed for long periods of time, and can be expected to move at maximum speed during exposure. Accurate correction of sight setting is seldom practicable. Firing should be opened at the existing sight setting, with corrections for range and wind applied by shifting the point of aim.

c. *Leads*.—Targets which cross the line of sight at any range are classified as crossing targets. In firing at such targets the firer must aim ahead of the target so that the paths of the target and bullet will meet. This distance ahead of the target is called the "lead." Targets which move directly toward the firer or directly away from him require no lead.

459353°—42——4   93

SECTION II

MOVING PERSONNEL

■ **64. TECHNIQUE.**—*a. Sight to be used.*—Under field conditions moving personnel present a fleeting target which is difficult to hit. This fact makes an accurate sight setting desirable. However, the fleeting character of these targets renders sight setting impractical. Up to the limiting range to 300 yards, any sight setting may be used for range, while the point of aim may be shifted into the wind for deflection. The soldier will be trained in this type of sight correction.

b. Method of aiming.—An elaborate system of calculating leads is neither necessary nor desirable. The following rules form the basis for estimating the proper leads. When firing at a man walking across or at right angles to the line of fire, the points of aim at the various ranges are—

(1) At 100 yards or less, aim at the *forward half* of his body.

(2) At 100 to 200 yards, aim at *forward edge* of his body.

(3) At 200 to 300 yards, lead him *one-half* the width of his body. Proficiency in this type of firing depends largely upon the amount of training the individual receives in aiming, squeezing the trigger, and leading with appropriate speed.

SECTION III

MOVING VEHICLES

■ **65. DETERMINATION AND APPLICATION OF LEADS.**—*a.* The lead necessary to hit a moving vehicle depends upon the speed of the target, the range to the target, and its direction of movement with respect to the line of sight. At 10 miles per hour, a vehicle travels approximately its own length (5 yards) in 1 second. A carbine bullet travels 300 yards in about ½ second. Therefore, to hit a vehicle moving at 10 miles an hour at a range of 300 yards, the lead should be 2½ yards, that is, ½ the target length or ½ lead.

b. Leads are applied by using the length of the target (as it appears to the firer) as the unit of measure. This eliminates the necessity for corrections due to the angle at which the target crosses the line of sight, because the more acute the angle the smaller the target appears and the less lateral speed it attains.

  c. The following lead table is furnished as a guide:

Target speed mph	100	200	300
10	Leading edge	¼	½
20	¼	½	¾
30	½	¾	1

■ 66. TECHNIQUE OF FIRE.—The following technique is suggested for firing at rapidly moving targets, using any sight setting up to 300 yards:

  a. *Approaching* or *receding targets.*—The firer holds his aim on the center of the target and squeezes off his shot.

  b. *Crossing targets.*—The firer alines his sights on the bottom of the target at its rearmost point, and swings straight across it to the estimated lead. The rifle is kept swinging and the shot squeezed off while the proper lead is maintained.

  c. *Rate of fire.*—Fire is delivered as rapidly as proper aiming permits.

■ 67. PLACE IN TRAINING.—The technique of firing at moving personnel and vehicles should follow instruction in known distance firing.

SECTION IV

MOVING TARGETS AND RANGES AND RANGE PRECAUTIONS

■ 68. MOVING TARGETS AND RANGES.—*a. Firing at moving personnel.*—Any class A range, or field range, is suitable for this purpose. E targets on sticks carried by men walking, running, and ducking provide excellent training. On the field range, targets on booms may be drawn from one pit to another. This training affords great scope for the ingenuity of the instructor.

  b. *Firing at moving vehicles.*—No elaborate set-up is required. A sled shown in figure 30 provides a satisfactory target. It may be towed by any vehicle in such a manner that the range from target to firer varies from 300 to 100 yards. No provision need be made for changing direction as the range is too short for maneuvering, but the courses towed by the towing vehicle should be varied.

■ 69. SAFETY PRECAUTIONS.—For general range precautions including danger areas, see AR 750–10. In addition to the

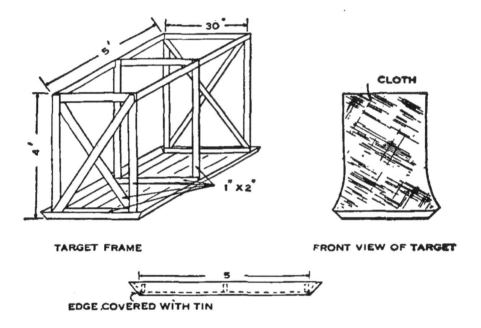

TARGET FRAME   FRONT VIEW OF TARGET

EDGE COVERED WITH TIN

ELEVATION OF BASE

FIGURE 30.—Target frame for moving target range.

individual safety precautions prescribed in section IX, chapter 1, the following precautions will be observed:

a. Firing at moving targets will not be permitted on any range until the safety angles have been carefully checked and markers have been placed so as to define clearly the right and left limits of fire.

b. Personnel of trucks towing targets will operate far enough from the line of fire to be protected not only from direct hits but also from ricochets.

c. Trucks replacing targets on the course, or personnel making repairs, will be equipped with red flags.

CHAPTER 4

MARKSMANSHIP—AIR TARGETS

SECTION I

AIR TARGETS FOR CARBINE

■ **70. GENERAL.**—The effectiveness of carbine fire against aircraft is far less than that of the rifle. For this reason, troops armed with the carbine will not fire on airplanes other than those delivering a low horizontal or dive-bombing attack. Enemy parachute troops while descending, and enemy gliders in the act of landing, are considered the primary aerial targets for personnel armed with the carbine, and the antiaerial training of this personnel will be such as to enable them to deliver effective fire on these targets.

■ **71. CLASSIFICATION.**—From the point of view of the man armed with the carbine, air targets may be classified as—
  a. Parachutists in the act of descent.
  b. Gliders in the act of descent.
  c. Airplanes passing overhead at low altitudes.
  d. Airplanes diving.

SECTION II

TECHNIQUE OF FIRE

■ **72. GENERAL.**—All aerial targets suitable for the carbine are fleeting in character, and fire must be opened promptly. Methods must be simple, and speed must be stressed. This section deals with actual fire on hostile targets. Details of marksmanship are contained in section III.

■ 73. LEADS.—*a. General.*—In order to hit a moving target, such as a parachutist, a glider, or an airplane in flight, it is necessary to aim an appropriate distance ahead of it and on its projected path so that the bullet and target will meet. This distance ahead of the target is called "lead." A lead must be applied in all firing except on the diving airplane.

b. Determination of leads.—(1) The lead necessary to engage a moving target depends upon—

(*a*) Speed of target.

(*b*) Range to target.

(*c*) Time of flight of bullet.

(*d*) Direction of flight of target with respect to line of fire.

(2) It is obviously impossible for a carbineer to consider the above factors, and to compute the required lead in the short time available to him. Therefore, leads are computed and placed in lead tables for the use of leaders in training their units. (See par. 73*d*.)

c. Application of leads.—Leads are tabulated in *apparent* target lengths. It is very difficult to estimate with any degree of accuracy a lead such as 15 yards or 30 yards at ranges from 100 to 300 yards. Therefore, the length of the target as it appears to the firer is used as the unit of measure for applying leads. The carbineer is trained to apply the length of the target, as it appears to him, along the projected path of the target to determine the aiming point for each shot.

d. Lead table.—The following lead table is furnished as a guide:

Slant range	Time of flight of bullet in seconds (approximate)	Lead required (target lengths)		
		Parachutist 6 feet high at 17 fps	Glider 40 feet long at 20 mph	Airplane 30 feet long at 250 mph
100	0. 17	½	0	2
200	. 43	1	½	5
300	. 70	2	¾	9

■ 74. DELIVERY OF FIRE.—*a. Range.*—(1) The maximum effective range of carbine fire at any target is 300 yards. However, carbineers should assume the firing position on receipt of warning of aerial attack, either by plane, parachute, or glider, and upon the approach of any such target they should start tracking. As the target comes within effective range, fire is opened.

(2) Range estimation is the product of experience. The firer bases his estimate on his knowledge of appearance of objects (gliders, parachutes, and planes) at known ranges. The following data are approximate:

> 300 yards____ The firer can plainly distinguish small parts of the plane or glider, and can identify portions of the parachutists' equipment.
>
> 200 yards____ All items of equipment carried by the parachutists are plainly visible. On planes and gliders, symbols, numbers and letters can be distinguished.

b. Rate of fire.—The rate of fire at aerial targets is about the same as rapid fire at ground targets. Experience indicates that an attempt to fire faster than is consistent with proper aim and trigger squeeze results in waste of ammunition. A well-trained carbineer can fire about one accurate shot each 2 seconds.

c. Sights.—The peep sight set at 300 yards is used.

Section III

MARKSMANSHIP TRAINING

■ 75. Instruction.—*a. Object.*—The object of aerial marksmanship instruction is to train the carbineer in the technique of firing at rapidly moving aerial targets.

b. Basis.—(1) Prior to instruction in aerial marksmanship, the soldier should have completed a course of training in ground firing and have acquired the fundamentals of good shooting. To become a good aerial marksman, he must be able to apply the fundamentals of target practice to firing at rapidly moving targets and to perform the following operations with accuracy and precision:

(a) Apply the length of the target as a unit of measure in measuring the required lead.

(b) Aline the sights of the carbine on the required lead rapidly.

(c) Swing the carbine with a smooth, uniform motion so as to maintain the aim on the required lead while getting off the shot.

(d) Apply continuous trigger squeeze so as to fire in a minimum of time and without disturbing the aim.

(2) The correct performance of these four operations combined into one continuous, smooth motion when firing in any direction at moving aerial targets is the basis of the course of training outlined herein.

c. *Sequence.*—Aerial marksmanship for the carbine is divided into preparatory exercises and miniature range practice.

d. *Personnel to receive training.*—All persons armed with the carbine should receive aerial marksmanship training.

■ 76. PREPARATORY EXERCISES. — a. *General.* — (1) *Description.*—The preparatory exercises are designed to teach the soldier the fundamentals of aerial marksmanship for the carbine, and to drill him therein until the correct procedure becomes a fixed habit. In addition to a brief explanation of the technique of aerial carbine fire, the preparatory exercises consist of the following two distinct steps which should be completed on targets as later indicated, prior to firing on those targets:

(a) Position exercise.

(b) Aiming, leading, and trigger squeeze exercises.

(2) *Method.*—A conference by the instructor should precede each exercise. This conference should include an explanation of the necessity of the exercise, and a demonstration by the instructor and a qualified squad. In order to awaken interest and stimulate the soldiers' enthusiasm, the preliminary instruction should be individual and thorough. Each man should understand and be able to explain each point.

(3) *Coaching.*—During all preparatory exercises and miniature range firing, when a man is in a firing position he should have a coach whose duty it is to watch him and point out his errors. For this purpose soldiers should be grouped in pairs and take turns in acting as coach and pupil. Unit

leaders are the instructors and should supervise and prompt the coaches.

b. Organization.—With the targets and target range described in paragraphs 82 and 84, a group of 32 men per target is the most economical training unit. For the preparatory exercises this will permit 16 men to perform the exercises on each type of target, while the remaining 16 men act as coaches. Each group should complete all preparatory training and instruction firing on its assigned target. Groups should then change places. The preparatory training and instruction firing should then be undertaken on the new type target.

■ 77. FIRST STEP—POSITION EXERCISES.—*a. General.*—The positions used in aerial target firing are those which can be assumed rapidly, which afford maximum flexibility to the body for manipulation of the carbine, and which do not require undue exposure of the firer. These positions will usually be either kneeling or standing. The kneeling position best meets the requirements listed above as it is less vulnerable than the standing position (fig. 31).

b. Firing positions.—(1) Aerial target firing positions differ from those used in ground firing in that—

(*a*) The arms are not supported, but move freely in any direction with the body.

(*b*) The hands grasp the piece firmly, the left hand near the upper band.

(*c*) The butt of the carbine is pressed firmly against the shoulder with the right hand, and the cheek is pressed against the stock.

(*d*) In the kneeling position the buttock does not rest on the heel, and the left foot is well advanced to the left front. The weight is slightly forward (see fig. 32).

(2) The positions must be such that the carbine, the body from the waist up, the arms, and the head are as one unit.

(3) When leading a target the firer swings the carbine with a smooth, uniform motion. This is done by pivoting the body at the waist. There should be no independent movement of the arms, head, shoulders, or the carbine.

(4) The instructor explains and demonstrates the position, and points out that if the carbine is pulled or pushed

FIGURE 31.—Standing antiaircraft firing position.

FIGURE 32.—Kneeling antiaircraft firing position.

in the desired direction by means of the left hand and arm the carbine will move with a jerky motion, thereby increasing the possibility of jerking the trigger, or the front sight may be pulled or pushed out of alinement with the rear sight and the eye.

(5) Position exercises should be conducted until the soldier becomes proficient in assuming positions rapidly for aerial firing in any direction.

■ 78. SECOND STEP—AIMING, LEADING, AND TRIGGER-SQUEEZE EXERCISE.—*a. Purpose.*—The purpose of this exercise is to teach the correct method of aiming, to develop skill in swinging the carbine with a smooth, uniform motion so as to maintain the correct aim on aerial targets, and to develop proper trigger squeeze.

b. Method.—(1) *Parachute target* (fig. 33①).—Pupils assigned to the parachute targets take up the ready position in one line at about 1½ yards interval, 500 inches from and facing their respective targets. Coaches take positions that enable them to observe their pupils. The commands for the exercise are: 1. AIMING AND LEADING EXERCISE, 2. ONE LEAD, 3. TARGETS. At the command TARGETS, the upper target is pulled down at a speed of approximately 1 foot per second; the pupils assume the designated position rapidly, aline the sights on the spotter indicating the proper lead, and swinging the carbine with a smooth, uniform motion of the body, maintain a steady aim on the spotter (see fig. 33① and ②). During this motion the trigger is squeezed steadily until the shot goes off; following the shot the motion is maintained, the trigger released, and another squeeze begun. During the 30 seconds of the target's descent, the firer endeavors to fire five simulated shots. When the target reaches the ground, coaches and pupils exchange places, the group on the other target of the pair, that is, the one now at the top, are readied, and the exercise repeated. The exercise is continued until all men have acquired skill in aiming, leading, and trigger squeeze.

(2) *Glider target.*—Firers assigned to the glider target are formed parallel to and 500 inches from the horizontal

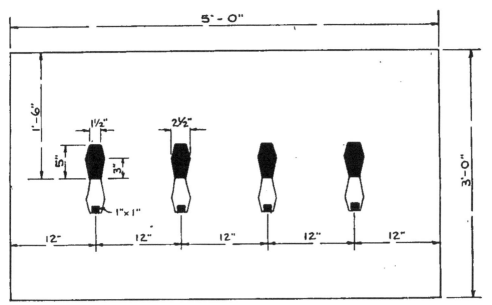

① Aiming and leading parachute target.

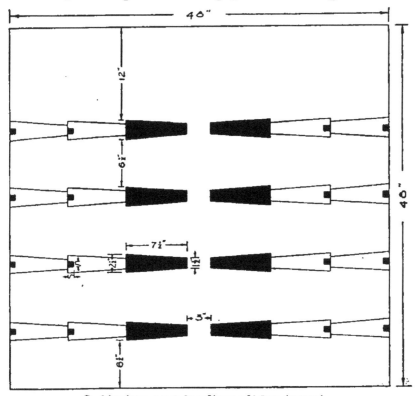

② Aiming and leading glider target.

FIGURE 33.

104

target as used for rifle antiaircraft fire (see fig. 34). The procedure is the same except as follows:

(a) Target is operated at a speed of 3 feet per second.

(b) Eight men of the firing group track the target in each direction.

(c) One and two leads are used.

c. *Importance of position, trigger squeeze, and follow-through.*—The importance of correct position and *the smooth swing* with constant trigger squeeze must be constantly emphasized.

d. *Duties of the coach.*—In this exercise the coach sees that the—

(1) Firer has taken the proper position.

(2) Trigger is squeezed steadily.

(3) Carbine is swung smoothly, with the arms, shoulders, carbine, and head moving as a unit.

(4) Eye is kept open and does not blink as the hammer falls.

(5) Muzzle does not jerk coincidentally with the release of the hammer.

(6) Aim is continuous during the entire length of travel of the target.

SECTION IV

MINIATURE RANGE PRACTICE

■ 79. GENERAL.—a. Miniature range practice is divided into two parts, instruction firing and group firing. There is no record firing.

b. All firing is on moving targets on the 500 inch range. A suggested arrangement of the range is given in paragraph 84. Provision is made for the simultaneous firing by two groups on the parachute and glider targets.

c. The course is fired with the carbine M1.

d. All carbines are targeted before range practice starts.

■ 80. SAFETY PRECAUTIONS.—a. Bolts of carbines should be open at all times except when on the firing line, firing, or simulating fire.

b. Carbines should be loaded only at the command of the officer in charge of the firing on each target.

c. At the completion of the firing of a score all carbines should be unloaded and bolts opened.

d. If firers go forward to inspect their targets, carbines should be left on the firing line.

e. No one will be permitted in advance of the firing line except by permission of the officer in charge of that particular target. He will not give such permission until he has assured himself that all carbines have been unloaded and the bolts are open.

f. Target operators will remain behind the protective wall except when ordered to leave by the officer in charge of the target which they are operating.

■ 81. INSTRUCTION FIRING.—*a. General.*—(1) The purpose of instruction firing is to provide a means of applying the principles taught in the preparatory exercises to actual firing.

(2) During instruction firing the coach-and-pupil method is followed.

(3) As a ·group completes preparatory training on a target, instruction firing should be taken up on that target and completed before the group moves to another target.

(4) Instruction firing consists of that indicated in table IV, paragraph 82.

b. Procedure.—(1) As the instruction firing on each type of target follows immediately after the preparatory exercises on that target, organization of the training unit should be in groups of 32 men (see par. 76*b*).

(2) Sixteen men of each group are formed on the firing line in the ready position. The remaining 16 men, in the rear rank, act as coaches.

(3) (*a*) On the parachute target one half of the firers fire on the right target of each frame, and one half on the left target.

(*b*) On the glider (horizontal) target one half of the firers fire while the target is moving from right to left, and the other half fires while it travels from left to right.

(*c*) Coaches and pupils exchange places after each string of 5 shots.

(4) All men not firing during a run of the target will simulate fire.

(5) Silhouettes are assigned to each firer. For example,

the four silhouettes on the right of the glider target are assigned to the first four men for the first run of the target. For the return (from left to right) the four silhouettes on the left of the target are assigned to the second four men. This procedure is followed four times until all men have fired a string, when coaches and pupils exchange places. On the parachute target the right frame is assigned the first and third groups of four; the left target to the second and fourth groups.

(6) The officer in charge of the target commands: 1. LOAD, 2 ONE (TWO) LEADS, 3. TARGETS. At the command TARGETS, the targets are operated at the proper speed. Men assigned silhouettes use the announced lead and attempt to fire 5 shots during the target run in the prescribed manner. Men not firing on any run will simulate fire on any silhouette.

(7) One point is scored for each hit in the proper scoring space or silhouette.

(8) Modifications of this method to meet local conditions are authorized.

■ 82. GROUP FIRING.—*a. General.*—(1) Group firing is the final phase of aerial marksmanship with the carbine.

(2) It provides competitions, and illustrates the effectiveness of the combined fire of a number of men armed with the carbine.

(3) Group firing should not be undertaken until the preparatory training and instruction firing have been completed.

b. Procedure.—(1) Two silhouettes on the glider target, one to be fired on from right to left, and one to be fired on from left to right, are assigned to each squad or similar group. On the parachute target one silhouette only is so assigned.

(2) Each man of the squad, in order as assigned, fires five rounds on each passage of the target.

(3) Targets are not scored until completion of the firing of each squad, or group.

c. Scoring.—1 point is scored for each hit in the proper scoring space on the silhouette.

TABLE IV.—*Instruction firing*
(Range 500 inches)

Target	Position		Total
	Kneeling	Standing	
Parachute_____	10	10	20
Glider_____	10	10	20
Total_____			40

SECTION V

RANGES, TARGETS, AND EQUIPMENT

■ 83. RANGE OFFICER.—A range officer is appointed well in advance of range practice. His chief duties are—

a. To make timely estimates for material and labor to place the range in proper condition for firing.

b. To supervise and direct the repairs and alterations to installations.

c. Where safety demands, to instruct and supervise range guards.

■ 84. MINIATURE RANGE.—a. The miniature range is that used for antiaircraft fire with the rifle, with the addition of the parachute target. It consists of—

(1) One glider (horizontal) target (fig. 34).

(2) Two parachute targets (fig. 35).

(3) The remaining targets are not used by troops armed with the carbine, and are not shown. They are described in FM 23–5, and illustrated therein by figure 42.

b. For details of range apparatus see figures 36, 37, and 38.

c. For danger space see AR 775–10.

■ 85. INDIVIDUAL SCORE CARD.

Target	Position		Percent of hits
	Kneeling	Standing	
Parachute_____			
Glider_____			

Average percent _____

CHAPTER 5
FIRING AT FIELD TARGETS

■ 86. CHARACTERISTICS OF FIRE.—The characteristics of the carbine determine the manner in which it is to be used. It is an individual weapon like the rifle, pistol, or revolver and was designed primarily to replace the pistol or revolver. It is highly effective at close quarters and at ranges up to 300 yards. Its 15-round magazine and semiautomatic action, together with its greater effective range, make it much superior to the pistol or revolver as a close-defense weapon. Men armed with the carbine are capable of dealing effectively with parachutists landing in their immediate vicinity, and with other hostile personnel encountered at ranges up to 300 yards. Carbineers are not organized into squads or other fire units, but deliver their fire as individuals. However, a small group of such personnel may be collected for the execution of group fire in situations where this action promises the best results. Carbines may be grouped with other available weapons, especially automatic rifles.

■ 87. TYPE OF FIRE ORDERS.—Except when firing is executed by a group of carbineers, fire orders are seldom necessary or desirable. When group firing is done the simplest type of fire order, giving the target and the command to commence or cease firing, is used.

■ 88. TARGET DESIGNATION.—The usual employment of the carbine is such that target designation, as employed for longer range weapons, is not necessary. Targets for such a close range weapon will generally be obvious. In most situations recognition of targets must be left to the carbineer.

■ 89. RANGE ESTIMATION.—*a. General.*—(1) The carbineer must be well trained in hasty range estimation and its application to marksmanship in the field. Because the maximum range for which the sights can be set in 300 yards and because the weapon is normally employed quickly at those ranges or under, the following methods of range estimation are used:

Estimation by eye.

Observation of fire.

(2) The usual method of range estimation is by eye. The carbineer is taught to estimate accurately and fix permanently

in his mind two distances, 50 yards and 100 yards.   Targets
at other ranges are estimated in comparison with these units
of measure.

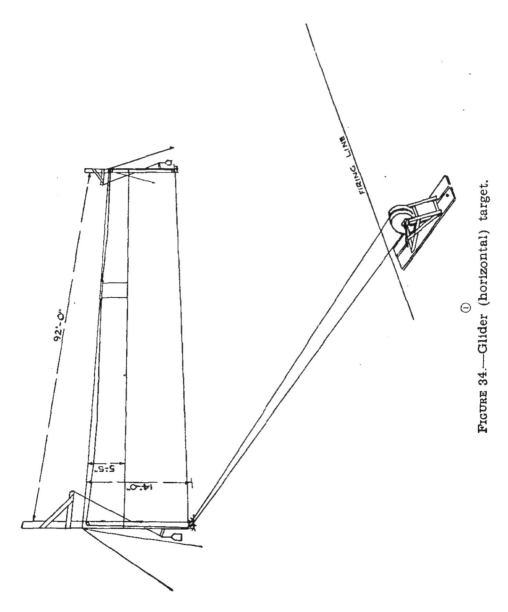

FIGURE 34.—Glider (horizontal) target.

(3) When the effect of a shot or series of shots can be
seen by the carbineer he corrects the range setting applied by
estimation in order to increase the effectiveness of his fire.

b. Exercises.—The following exercises can be used as guides in instructing the carbineer in range estimation. Ranges used are short and at no time greater than 300 yards. The exercises are especially suitable for class instruction.

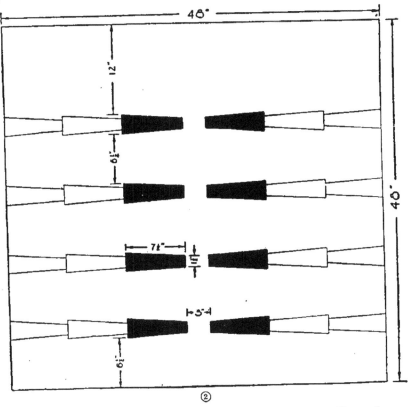

FIGURE 34.—Glider (horizontal) target—Continued.

(1) No. 1.—(*a*) *Purpose.*—To familiarize the carbineer with the units of measure, 50 yards and 100 yards.

(*b*) *Method.*—The units of measure, 50 yards and 100 yards, are staked out on the ground up to 300 yards. The carbineer is required to become familiar with the appearance of the unit of measure from the prone, kneeling, and standing positions.

(2) No. 2.—(*a*) *Purpose.*—To give practice in range estimation.

(*b*) *Method.*—From a suitable point, ranges are previously

111

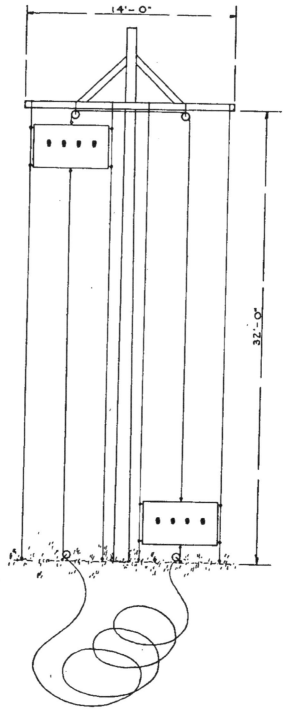

① Parachute target.

FIGURE 35.

measured to normal targets within 300 yards.   The carbineer
is required to estimate the ranges to the various objects as
they are pointed out by the instructor and record his estima-

② Parachute silhouettes.

FIGURE 35—Continued.

tion on a sheet of paper.   At least one-half of the estimates
are made from the kneeling and sitting positions..   Thirty

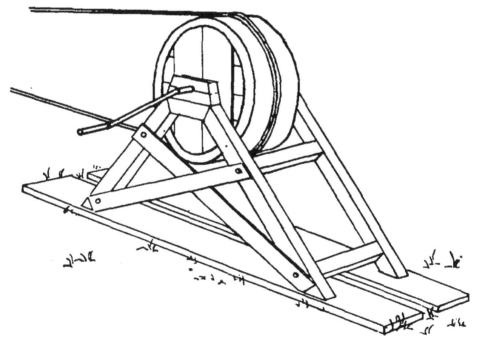

FIGURE 36.—Details of construction of operating drum.

seconds are allowed for each estimate.   When all the ranges
have been estimated the paper is checked by the instructor,
and the true ranges given to the student.

113

c. Appearance of objects.—If much of the ground between the observer and the target is hidden from view, he estimates the range by the appearance of objects. Whenever the ap-

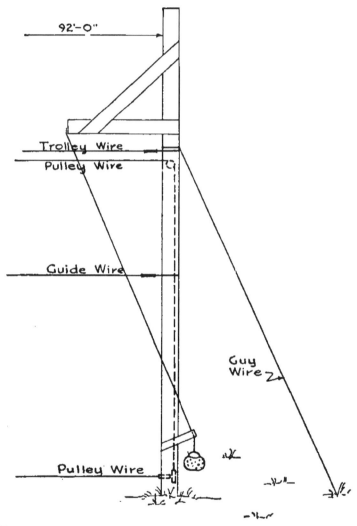

92'-0"

Trolley Wire
Pulley Wire

Guide Wire

Guy
Wire

Pulley Wire

FIGURE 37.—Details of construction of horizontal target support
and bumper.

pearance of objects is used as a basis for range estimation, the observer must make allowance for the following effects:
   (1) Objects seem nearer—
   (a) When the object is in a bright light.

(b) When the color of the object contrasts sharply with the color of the background.

(c) When looking over water, snow, or a uniform surface like a wheat field.

(d) When looking downward from a height.

(e) In the clear atmosphere of high altitudes.

(f) When looking over a depression, most of which is hidden.

(2) Objects seem more distant—

(a) When looking over a depression most of which is visible.

(b) When there is a poor light or fog.

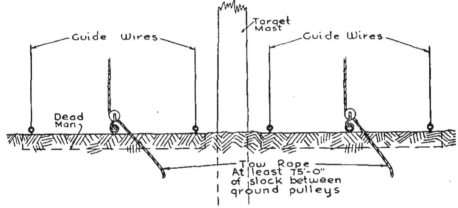

FIGURE 38.—Details of construction of parachute target.

(c) When only a small part of the object can be seen.

(d) When looking from low ground upward toward higher ground.

d. If the carbine is equipped with an adjustible sight, the sights are set to correspond to the estimated range. If the L-type sight is used the correct aiming point at the various distances as determined during marksmanship training is used. .

■ 90. TRAINING IN FIELD FIRING.—a. Upon completion of marksmanship practice, firing at field targets will be done by all individuals armed with the carbine.

b. This firing is done by groups. The size of the group will depend upon the number of men to fire and the range facilities available. Usually the size of the area and safety requirements will not permit the firing of more than 20 men at one time.

■ 91. FIELD FIRING RANGE.—The known distance range, class B range, or any other suitable area may be used for firing at field targets. It is desirable to select an area which will permit the advance of the firers and allow firing at ranges from 200 to 50 yards.

■ 92. FIELD FIRING COURSE.—The following field target firing course is given as a guide and may be modified to suit range facilities, equipment, ammunition and time available. (See fig. 39.)

a. On a known distance range, class B range, or other suitable area, partially concealed prone silhouettes (E targets) are placed in groups of three in an irregular line with intervals of about 5 yards between targets and about 20 yards between groups.

b. The men to fire are formed in line about 200 yards from the targets so that each man is opposite the center of his assigned targets. Each man has two magazines, one containing 6 and one 12 rounds. Carbines are carried at the "ready," loaded, and locked.

c. The officer in charge of firing, from a position in rear of the center of the line, commands or signals: FORWARD MARCH, and himself moves forward behind the advancing line. The advance from the initial point is at a walk. At a whistle signal given by the officer in charge the men take the sitting position and fire or attempt to fire 2 rounds at each of their targets. After 20 seconds the signal to cease firing is given, and the advance resumed at double time toward the next firing position. Upon signal the men halt and fire a similar score from the kneeling position. After 20 seconds the advance is resumed at a run to the next firing position and the final score fired from the standing position.

d. To add interest and instructional value the distance of each advance should vary but in no case should exceed 50 yards.

e. Carbines are locked and carried at the "ready" while advancing. When the firing signal is given men individually unlock pieces, assume the prescribed firing position, and engage their targets.

f. Limits of each group of targets are indicated by flags or other means, so that each firer will fire on his own targets.

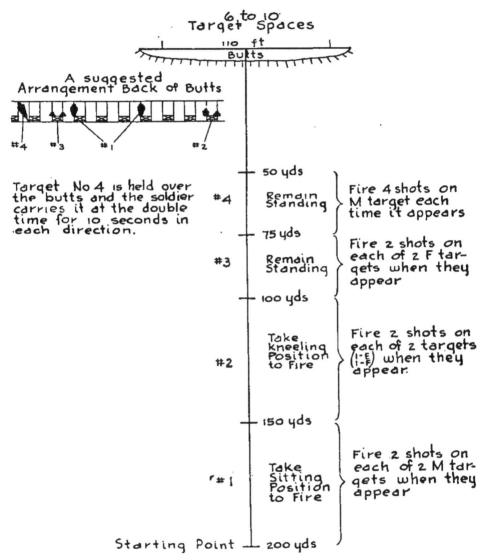

FIGURE 39—Field firing course.

g. To enforce safety precautions the officer in charge should have several noncommissioned assistants distributed in rear of the line and following it during firing. The number required will depend on the extent of the line. These

117

assistants prevent individuals from getting ahead of or behind the general line and see that loaded pieces are locked and kept pointed toward the targets during the advance.

h. Upon completion of the firing carbines are unloaded. Firers move forward, inspect their targets, assist in scoring, and paste their targets.

i. Should a difficult stoppage occur during the course of firing the man concerned continues forward with the rest of the group and reduces the stoppage when the course is finished.   If practicable he should reduce the stoppage during the firing and continue with the rest of the group.   He must not, however, be permitted to lag behind the general line of men for this purpose.

■ 93. SCORING.—To stimulate interest and competition, scores are kept for all firing and are posted where participants can see them.   The following system of scoring is suggested:

<pre>
For each hit_____   4
    Total possible for hits_____ 18 x 4=72
Bonus for hitting all targets_____   10
Bonus for hitting all targets 6 times_____   18
                                                     ───
    Total possible _____   100
</pre>

CHAPTER 6

ADVICE TO INSTRUCTORS

SECTION I

GENERAL

■ 94. PURPOSE.—The provisions of this chapter are to be accepted as a guide and not as having the force of regulations. They are particularly applicable to emergency conditions when large bodies of troops are being trained under officers and noncommissioned officers who are not thoroughly familiar with approved training methods.

SECTION II

MECHANICAL TRAINING

■ 95. CONDUCT OF TRAINING.—*a.* As a general rule instruction is so conducted as to insure the uniform progress of the unit.

b. The instructor briefly explains the subject to be taken up and demonstrates it himself or with a trained assistant.

c. The instructor then causes one man in each squad or subgroup to perform the step while he again explains it.

d. The instructor next causes all members of the squads or subgroups to perform the step, checked by their noncommissioned officers. This is continued until all men are proficient in the particular operation, or until those whose progress is slow have been placed under special instructors.

e. Subsequent steps are taken up in like manner during the instruction period.

SECTION III

MARKSMANSHIP—KNOWN-DISTANCE TARGETS

■ 96. GENERAL.—*a.* Training is preferably organized and conducted as outlined in paragraphs 45 and 46. Officers should generally be considered as the instructors of their units. As only one step is taken up at a time, and as each step begins with a lecture and a demonstration showing exactly what to do, the trainees, although not previously instructed, can carry on the work under the supervision of the instructor.

b. It is advisable that units be relieved from routine garrison duty during the period of preparatory marksmanship training and range practice.

■ 97. PLACE OF ASSEMBLY FOR LECTURES.—Any small ravine or cup-shaped area makes a good amphitheater for giving the lecture in case no suitable building is available.

■ 98. ASSISTANT INSTRUCTIONS.—a. It is advantageous to have all officers and as many noncommissioned officers as possible trained in advance in the prescribed methods of instruction. When units are undergoing marksmanship training for the first time, this is not always practicable nor is it absolutely necessary. A good instructor can give a clear idea of how to carry on the work in his lecture and demonstration preceding each step. In the supervision of the work following the demonstration, he can correct any mistaken ideas or misinterpretations.

b. When an officer in charge of carbine instruction (see par. 46) is conducting successive organizations through target practice, it is advisable to attach to the first organization taking the course officers and noncommissioned officers of the organizations that are to follow for the period of preparatory work and for a few days of range firing. These act as assistant instructors when their own units take up the work. These assistants are particularly useful when one group is firing on the range and another is going through the preparatory exercises, both under the supervision of one instructor.

■ 99. EQUIPMENT.—The instructor should personally inspect the equipment for the preparatory exercises before the training begins. A set of model equipment should be prepared in advance by the instructor for the information and guidance of the organization about to take up the preparatory work. The sighting bars must be made as described, and the hole representing the peep sight must be absolutely circular. If the sights are made of tin the holes should be bored by a drill. Good rear sights can be made for the sighting bars by using cardboard and cutting the holes with a punch for cutting wads for 10-gage shotgun shells. Bull's-eyes painted on a white disk are not satisfactory. Bull's-eyes cut out of black paper with a shotgun-wad cutter and pasted on white paper make satisfactory aiming points either to paste on the face of the disk or to use in position and trigger-squeeze exercises when small gallery targets are not available for this purpose.

■ 100. INSPECTION OF CARBINES.—No man is required to fire with an unserviceable or inaccurate carbine. All carbines should be carefully inspected far enough in advance of the period of training to permit organization commanders to replace all inaccurate or defective carbines. Carbines having badly pitted barrels are not accurate and should not be used.

■ 101. AMMUNITION.—The best ammunition available should be reserved for record firing, and the men should have a chance to learn their sight settings with that ammunition before record practice begins. Ammunition of different makes and of different lots should not be used indiscriminately.

■ 102. ORGANIZATION.—*a. In preparatory training.*—(1) The field upon which the preparatory work is to be given should be selected in advance and a section of it assigned to each organization The equipment and apparatus for the work should be on the ground and in place before the morning lecture is given, so that each organization can move to its place and begin work immediately and without confusion.

(2) Each company should be organized in two lines facing away from each other. In this way the officers and other instructors, whose position is normally between the lines, have all of their squads under close supervision. In figure 40 the groups represented consist of 8 men each.

(3) The arrangement of the equipment is as follows:

(a) On each line are placed the sighting bars and carbine rests at sufficient intervals to permit efficient work.

(b) Fifty feet from each line is placed a line of small boxes with blank paper tacked on one side, one box and one small sighting disk to each carbine rest.

(c) Two hundred yards from each line is placed a line of

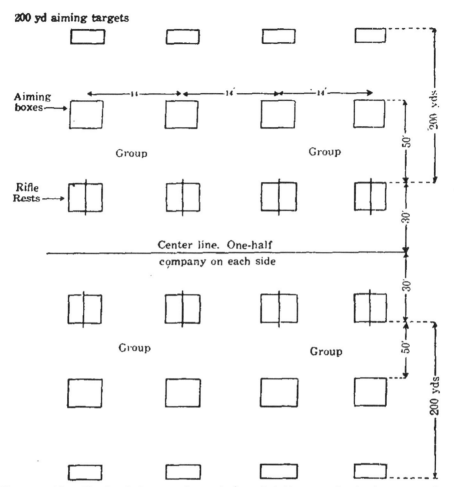

FIGURE 40.—Part of field laid out for sighting and aiming exercises.

frames suitable for 200-yard shot group exercises, one frame to each squad. These frames have blank paper tacked or pasted on the front. A 10-inch sighting disk is placed with each frame. Machine-gun targets make acceptable frames for this work.

(4) In position, trigger-squeeze, and rapid-fire exercises targets should be placed at 1,000 inches and 200 yards. The groups represented in figure 41 consist of 8 men each.

(5) When sufficient level ground is not available for the above arrangement the organizations will have to vary from it in some particulars. It will usually be found, however, that all of the work except the long-range shot group work can be carried on in two lines.

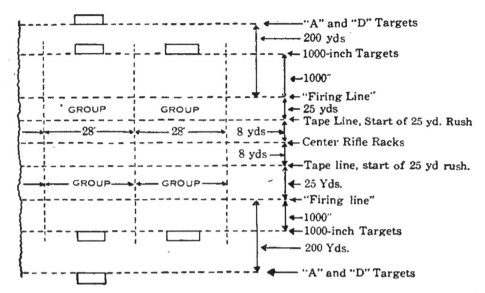

FIGURE 41.—Part of field laid out for position, trigger squeeze, and rapid fire exercises.

b. In range practice.—(1) The range work should be so organized that there is a minimum of lost time on the part of each man. Long periods of inactivity while awaiting a turn on the firing line should be avoided. For this reason the number of men on the range should be accommodated to the number of targets available.

(2) As a general rule six men per target are about the maximum and four men per target the minimum for efficient handling.

(3) Subject to ammunition allowances, the following method of carrying on range practice has been found to produce uniformly excellent results when the full allowance of time is devoted to the training:

(*a*) Firing is begun by a group consisting of approximately half of each organization. This group is made up of those proved to be the best by the examination on preparatory work and those known to be good shots. The men who are not included in this first group make up all fatigue details and undergo additional preparatory training.

(*b*) At the completion of instruction practice, all of the first group, except those few who have not been shooting well, fire for record.

(*c*) When the first group has completed firing, the second

123

group, made up of those who have not fired and those who were rejected from the first group begin their firing. The men who have completed record firing perform all fatigue.

(*d*) At the completion of instruction practice, all of this second group who have been shooting well and have a very good chance to qualify fire for record.

(*e*) During the remainder of the allotted time the efforts of the officers and noncommissioned officers are concentrated on the men who were not ready to fire for record with the second group. This last group must complete firing for record by the end of the allotted time for range practice.

(4) When range facilities are such that the entire organization can fire at one time without having more than six men per target, the same general scheme as that outlined above may be applied. The details of this plan follow:

(*a*) Firing is begun with all of the men of the organization taking part.

(*b*) At the completion of instruction practice, all except those who have not been shooting well fire for record.

(*c*) The efforts of the instructors are concentrated on the remainder of the organization for the rest of the allotted time.

■ 103. MODEL SCHEDULES.—The following schedule of preparatory exercises and practice firing is suggested as a guide:

(1) *For men who have recently completed a course in rifle marksmanship.*—This schedule is based on a 14-hour course. The practice firing is based on a maximum of six orders per target, or pair of two targets.

FIRST DAY	*Hours*	
	AM	PM
Review of sighting and aiming exercises_____	1	
Position exercises (¼ hour in each position)_____	1	
Trigger squeeze exercises (½ hour in each position)___	2	
Zeroing rifles, instruction practice (table II)_____		4

SECOND DAY		
Instruction practice (simulated), table III_____	2½	
Instruction practice, table III_____	1½	
Instruction practice (simulated), table III_____		1½
Record practice, table III_____		1½

(2) *For men who have not had a course in rifle marksmanship.*—This schedule is based on a 39 hour course. The

practice and record firing is based on a maximum of six orders per target, or pair of targets.

FIRST DAY

	Hours	
	AM	PM
MECHANICAL TRAINING_____	¾	
FIRST STEP: Sighting and aiming exercises_____	¼	
First sighting and aiming exercise_____:_____	½	
Sight blackening and second sighting and aiming exercise_____	½	
Third sighting and aiming exercise to include long range shot group exercise_____	1½	
Safety precautions_____	½	
SECOND STEP: Position exercises.		
Holding breath, trigger slack, general rules for positions _____		1*
Position exercise.		
Prone _____		½ *
Sitting_____		½ *
Kneeling_____		½ *
Standing_____		½ *

*This period should be conducted so that the practical work in each position is preceded by a 15-minute lecture and demonstration of that position.

SECOND DAY

	AM	PM
THIRD STEP: Trigger squeeze exercises_____	½	
Prone_____	½	
Sitting_____	½	
Kneeling_____	½	
Standing_____	½	
Assuming positions rapidly_____	½	
Practical work assuming positions rapidly (all positions) _____	1	
FOURTH STEP: Rapid fire exercises_____		½
Standing to prone (simulate firing, table II, 300 yards) _____		½
Standing and sitting (simulate firing, table II, 200 yards) _____		½
Standing and kneeling (simulate firing, table II, 200 yards) _____		½
Standing and kneeling (simulate firing, table II, 100 yards) _____		1

THIRD DAY

	AM	PM
FIFTH STEP: Sight settings, aiming points, and scorebook_____	½	
Scorebook exercises_____	½	
Trigger squeeze exercises (all positions slow fire) __	1	
Rapid fire exercises (all positions) _____	1	
Examination of all men by group instructors_____	1	
Instruction practice slow fire (table I)_____		3

FOURTH DAY

	AM	PM
Instruction practice (simulated), table II (all positions) _____	½	
Instruction practice, Table II_____	3½	
Instruction practice (simulated), table III_____		1
Instruction practice, table III_____		2

FIFTH DAY

Instruction practice, table II_____ 3½
Instruction practice (simulated), table III_____ ½
Instruction practice (simulated), table III_____   1½
Instruction practice, table III_____   1½

SIXTH DAY

Instruction practice (simulated), table III_____ 1½
Record practice_____ 1½

■ 104. LECTURES AND DEMONSTRATIONS.—*a.* The lectures at the beginning of each step are an important part of the instruction methods. The lectures may be given to the assembled group undergoing preparatory training up to and including a group formed into a provisional battalion or body of recruits of similar size. However, when the men of a battalion formed into a provisional company take up carbine training, the talks and demonstrations as a rule are made by the officer designated to conduct the training. It is not necessary that the lecturers be expert shots.

b. The notes on lectures which follow are to be used merely as a guide. The points which usually require elucidation and demonstration are placed in side headings in italics. The notes which follow each heading are merely to assist the instructor in preparing his lecture. The lecturer should know in advance what he is going to say on the subject. Under no circumstances will he read over to a class the outlines for lectures contained herein, nor will he read a lecture prepared by himself. During the lecture the headings in italics, jotted down as notes, serve as a guide to the order in which the points are to be discussed. If he cannot talk interestingly and instructively on each subject without elaborate notes, he should not give the lectures at all.

c. It is important to show the men undergoing instruction, by explanation and demonstration, just how to go through the exercises and to tell them why they are given these exercises.

■ 105. FIRST LECTURE—SIGHTING AND AIMING.—*a.* The class is assembled in a building or natural amphitheater in the open where all can hear the instructor and see the demonstrations.

b. The following equipment is necessary:
    1 sighting bar.
    1 carbine rest.

1 carbine.

1 small sighting disk.

1 long range sighting disk.

1 small box.

Material for blackening sights.

c. The following subjects are usually discussed in the first lecture:

(1) *Value of knowing how to shoot.*—(a) The carbine is the close-protection weapon of the individual in war. Expertness in its use gives the individual confidence and a higher morale.

(b) Individual proficiency increases the efficiency of the organization as a whole.

(c) Carbine firing is good sport.

(2) *Object of target practice.*—(a) To teach men how to shoot.

(b) To show them how to teach others.

(c) To train future instructors.

(3) *Training to shoot well.*—(a) Any man can be taught to shoot well. Shooting is a purely mechanical operation which can be taught to anyone physically fit to be a soldier.

(b) It requires no inborn talent.

(c) There are only a few simple things to do in order to shoot well, but these things must be done exactly right. If they are done only approximately right the result will be poor.

(4) *Method of instruction.*—(a) The method of instruction is the same as that used in teaching any mechanical operation.

(b) The instruction is divided into steps. The man is taught each step and practices it before going to the next step. When he has been taught all of the steps he is taken to the range to apply what he has learned.

(c) If he has been properly taught the various preparatory steps, he will do good shooting from the very beginning of range practice.

(d) Explain coach-and-pupil method and why used.

(5) *Reflecting attitude of instructor.*—If the instructor is interested, enthusiastic, and energetic, the men will be the same. If the instructor is inattentive, careless, and bored, the men will be the same, and the scores will be low.

(6) *Examination of men on preparatory work.*—Each man is examined in the preparatory work before going to the range. An outline of this examination is given in paragraph 53.

(7) *Method of marking blank form.*—Explain blank form (par. 46*f*). Explain marking system by the use of a blackboard if available.

(8) *Five essentials to good shooting.*—(*a*) Correct sighting and aiming.

(*b*) Correct position.

(*c*) Correct trigger squeeze.

(*d*) Correct application of rapid-fire principles.

(*e*) Knowledge of proper sight and aiming-point adjustments.

(9) *Today's work.*—First step—sighting and aiming.

(10) *Demonstration of first sighting-and-aiming exercise.*—Have a squad on stage or platform show just how this exercise is carried on.

(11) *Blackening the sights.*—Explain why this is done, and demonstrate how.

(12) *Demonstration of second sighting-and-aiming exercise.*—Assume that some of the squad have qualified in the first exercise. Put these men through the second sighting-and-aiming exercise and show just how it is done.

(13) *Demonstration of third sighting-and-aiming exercise.*—(*a*) Assume that some of the squad have qualified in the second sighting-and-aiming exercise. Put these men through the third sighting-and-aiming exercise and show just how it is done.

(*b*) Show how the squad is organized for the coach-and-pupil method so as to keep each man busy all the time.

(14) *Long-range shot group work.*—Show the class the disk for 100-yard shot group work. Explain how this work is carried on and why. Show some simple system of signals that may be used.

(15) *Final word.*—(*a*) Start keeping your blank form today.

(*b*) Organize your work so that all men are busy at all times.

(16) Are there any questions?

(17) Next lecture will be_____(state hour and place).

■ 106. SECOND LECTURE—POSITION.—*a.* The following equipment is necessary for the demonstrations in this lecture:

    1 carbine.

    1 box with small aiming target.

b. The following subjects are usually discussed in the second lecture:

(1) *Importance of each step.*—(*a*) Each step includes all that has preceded.

(*b*) Each step must be thoroughly learned and practiced or the instruction will not be a success.

(2) *Necessity for correct positions.*—No excellent shot varies from the normal positions. Few men with poor positions are even fair shots. Few men with good positions are poor shots. Instruction in positions involves correct aiming.

(3) *Taking up slack.*—Show the class the slack on the trigger. Explain why it is taken up in the position exercises. (Cannot begin to squeeze the trigger until the slack has been taken up.)

(4) *Holding breath.*—Explain the correct manner of holding the breath and have the class practice it a few times. Explain how the coach observes the pupil's breathing by watching his back.

(5) *Position of thumb.*—May be either over the, stock or on top of the stock but never along the *side of* the stock. Explain why.

(6) *Joints of finger.*—Trigger may be pressed with first or second joint; second joint is preferable when it can be done conveniently.

(7) *Prone position.*—(*a*) Demonstrate correct prone position, calling attention to the elements which go to make up a correct prone position: body at the correct angle, legs spread well apart, position of the butt on the shoulder, position of the hands on the carbine, position of cheek against the stock, position of elbows.

(*b*) Mention the usual faults which occur in prone position.

(*c*) Demonstrate the correct position again.

(8) *Sitting position.*—Demonstrate in the same manner as described above for the prone position.

(9) *Kneeling position.*—Demonstrate in the same manner as described for the prone position.

(10) *Standing position.*—Demonstrate in the same manner as described above for the prone position.

(11) *Today's work—position exercises.*—(a) Demonstrate the duties of a coach in a position exercise, calling attention to each item.

(b) Demonstrate the position of the coach. Always placed so that he can watch the pupil's finger and eye.

(c) Place a squad on an elevated platform and show how the squad leader organizes it by employing the coach-and-pupil method so as to keep every man occupied.

(d) Continue the long-range triangle work today.

(12) *Do not squeeze trigger today.*—Take up the slack in these exercises but do not squeeze the trigger.

(13) *Keep blank forms up-to-date.*—Examine each man in the squad at the end of the day's work and assign him a mark.

(14) Are there any questions?

(15) Next lecture will be _____ (state hour and place).

■ 107. THIRD LECTURE—TRIGGER SQUEEZE.—*a.* The following equipment is necessary for demonstration:

    1 carbine.

    1 box with small aiming target.

b. The following subjects are usually discussed in the third lecture:

(1) *Trigger squeeze most important.*—Read paragraph 50. Explain that there is only one correct method of squeezing the trigger—a steady increase of pressure so that the firer does not know when the explosion will take place. Emphasize the fact that this method of squeezing the trigger secures good results and must be applied in rapid fire.

(2) *Machine rest example.*—Lay the carbine on a table pointing down the room toward an actual or imaginary target; assume that it is in a machine rest which runs on a track parallel to the line of targets; assume that you fire a shot which hits the left edge of a 20-inch bull's-eye, 300 yards away; then move the rifle 20 inches to the right on the table as if it were sliding along the parallel track and assume that another shot is fired. Where does it hit? Answer: The right edge of the bull's-eye. Move the rifle back-

ward and forward between these two positions, and assume a shot is fired anytime while it is moving. Where will it hit? Answer: In the bull's-eye. Now assume that you hold the butt of the rifle still and move the muzzle a fraction of an inch. Where will it hit? Answer: It will miss the whole target. It hits the target when the whole rifle moves but misses it when only one end moves.

(3) *Pulsations of body.*—The natural movements of the body and its pulsations produce more or less parallel movement of the carbine. Often men who are apparently very unsteady make good scores. You thus see that if you squeeze the trigger so as not to know when the carbine will go off, the shot is displaced only by the amount of the parallel movement and will be a good one. But if you give the trigger a sudden jerk you deflect one end of the carbine and the shot will be a poor one.

(4) *Aim and hold.*—Any man can easily learn to hold a good aim for 15 to 20 seconds, which is a much longer period than is necessary to fire a well-aimed shot. Poor shots are usually the men who spoil their aim when they fire.

(5) *Coach squeezing trigger.*—(a) The fact that when the coach squeezes the trigger for the firer the shot is almost invariably a good one proves that poor shooting is principally due to errors in the trigger squeeze.

(b) By watching the firer's back the coach knows when the firer is aiming and then presses steadily on the trigger. Demonstrate how it is done.

(6) *When carbine goes off before man is ready.*—Often a man who has been doing poor shooting will state upon firing a shot, "I cannot call that shot. It went off before I was ready." Almost invariably these shots are well-placed. His poor shooting has been caused by "getting ready" for them.

(7) *Calling shot.*—Explain calling the shot and why it is done.

(8) *Today's work—trigger-squeeze exercise.*—(a) Demonstrate the duties of a coach in a trigger-squeeze exercise by calling attention to each item.

(b) The work is carried on as in position exercises with the squeezing of the trigger added.

(c) Practice only in the prone position this morning.

(d) Finish up the long-range shot group work today.

(9) *Keep blank form up to date.*—Examine each man in the squad at the end of the day's work and assign him a mark.

(10) *Final word.*—Do not let yourselves become bored with this work. It is easy to learn, but it takes a lot of practice to train the muscles and to get in the habit of doing the right thing without thinking.

(11) Are there any questions?

(12) Next lecture will be_____(state hour and place).

■ 108: FOURTH LECTURE—RAPID FIRE.—*a.* The following equipment is necessary for the demonstrations:

    1 carbine.

b. The following subjects are usually discussed in the fourth lecture:

(1) *Rapid fire true test of good shot.*—Superiority of fire in battle depends on the ability to deliver rapid and accurate fire.

(2) *Trigger squeeze same as in slow fire.*

(3) *Meaning of rapid fire.*—Rapid fire is merely continuous fire. The rapidity comes from the development of timing, reloading the magazines smoothly, and keeping the eye on the target.

(4) *Keeping eye on target.*—Explain the advantages of this and how it gains time.

(5) *Application in war.*—Explain the advantage of keeping eye on the target in combat.

(6) *Timing exercise.*—(*a*) Explain timing in rapid fire.

(*b*) Demonstrate timing.

(7) *Operation of bolt in rapid-fire exercise.*—Show how the coach presses the operating handle with a sharp motion, and then releases the pressure to permit the operating handle to go forward each time the pupil squeezes the trigger in the prone, sitting, and in the kneeling positions. Call attention to the details in each case.

(8) *Necessity for rapid-fire practice.*—A natural rhythm in firing on the part of a soldier materially increases his rapid-fire scores and his efficiency in battle.

(9) *Assuming positions rapidly.*—(a) The prone position can be assumed and an aimed shot fired more rapidly than from any other position.

(b) Application in combat.

(c) Demonstrate rapid-fire exercises, standing to prone, standing to kneeling, and standing to sitting, first by the numbers and then as one smooth movement.

(d) Even if it takes a few seconds longer, get into the correct position before starting to shoot.

(10) *Today's work—rapid fire exercise.*—(a) Explain how exercises are to be carried on.

(b) Demonstrate the duties of a coach in a rapid-fire exercise, calling attention to each item.

(11) *Keep blank forms up to date.*—Examine each man in the squad at the end of the day's work and assign him a mark.

(12) Are there any questions?

(13) Next lecture will be _____ (state hour and place).

■ 109. Fifth Lecture—Effect of Wind and Light; Sight Changes; Score Book.—*a.* This part of the preparatory instruction can be given on any day in which the weather forces the work to be done indoors. If no bad weather occurs, this work should follow rapid-fire instruction.

b. The following equipment is necessary for the demonstrations:

(1) One A and B target and an A and B target center for each range at which each of these targets is to be used in range practice. These targets are to be mounted on a frame.

(2) Eight spotters that can readily be stuck into the target.

(3) Each man to have his carbine and a scorebook.

c. The following subjects are usually discussed in the fifth lecture:

(1) *Targets.*—Explain the divisions on the target, and the target centers and give the dimensions of each.

(2) *Weather conditions.*—All weather conditions disregarded except wind.

(3) *Wind.*—(a) Explain how the direction of the wind is described.

(b) Explain how the velocity of the wind is estimated.

(c) Explain the effect of wind. Effect increases with distance from target.

(4) *Windage for first shot.*—State windage rule and explain it.

(5) *Elevation.*—State rule and explain it.

(6) *Shooting up or down hill.*—Explain the effect on elevation.

(7) *Scorebook.*—(a) Explain the uses of scorebook on range.

(b) Have class open scorebooks and explain items of keeping a score point by point.

(8) *Exercises.*—Give the class a number of small problems as a demonstration as to how the day's work is to be carried on.

(9) *This period.*—(a) Study and practice sight setting, sight and aiming-point changes, and the use of scorebook.

(b) Additional practice in the exercises of the preceding days and rapid-fire exercises.

(10) Are there any questions?

(11) Next lecture will be ------------------ (state hour and place).

■ 110. SIXTH LECTURE—RANGE PRACTICE.—This lecture and demonstration should immediately precede range firing. If the class is not too large, it should be given on a firing point of the rifle range.

a. The following equipment is necessary for the demonstrations:

    1 carbine.

    Material for blackening sight.

b. The following subjects are usually discussed in the sixth lecture:

(1) *Preparatory work applied.*—Range practice is carried on practically the same as a trigger-squeeze exercise except that ball cartridges are used.

(2) *Coaching.*—Coach watches the man not the target. Coach does not keep the score for the pupil. Pupil must make his own entries in his scorebook. Coach sees that he does this.

(3) *Officers and noncommissioned officers.*—(a) Supervise and prompt the men acting as coaches.

(b) Personally coach pupils who are having difficulty in making good scores.

(4) *Spotters.*—(a) Use in both slow and rapid fire.

(b) If a spotter near the edge of the bull's-eye bothers the pupil in aiming, it may be removed before he fires again.

(5) *Watching the eye.*—Explain how this indicates whether or not the pupil is squeezing the trigger properly.

(6) *Position of coach.*—Demonstrate in each one of the positions.

(7) *Demonstration of coaching in slow fire.*—(a) Place a man on the firing point and show just what a coach does, by calling attention to each item. (See par. 58e.)

(b) Demonstrate coach squeezing the trigger for pupil.

(8) *Demonstration of coaching in rapid fire.*—Same procedure as in paragraph 58e(7).

(9) *Read final precautions for slow fire.*—See paragraph 58c.

SECTION IV

MARKSMANSHIP—AIR TARGETS

■ 111. PRELIMINARY PREPARATION.—a. The officer in charge of aerial target training should be thoroughly familiar with the subject; should have detailed sufficient officers as assistant instructors;· and should train the assistant instructors and a demonstration group before the first training period.

b. He should inspect the range and equipment in sufficient time prior to the first training period to permit correction of deficiencies.

■ 112. DESCRIPTION OF MINIATURE RANGE.—a. *Targets.*—(1) *Glider.*—This target is designed to represent a glider flying parallel to the firing point.

(2) *Parachute.*—This target is in two sections each of two balanced targets, one of which is used on each run. Each frame contains four conventionalized silhouettes five inches high, below which is a similar recording (blank) silhouette. The target is operated at a speed of descent of 1 foot per second, which corresponds approximately to the angular travel of a parachutist descending 17 feet per second at a range of 300 yards.

135

b. Size and speed of silhouette.—The black silhouette is a representation at 500 inches of a proper target at a range of 300 yards. The speed of the silhouettes should be 3 feet and 1 foot per second. These speeds represent a glider flying between 20 and 25 miles per hour at a range of 300 yards and a parachutist dropping at a rate of 17 feet per second.

■ 113. PREPARATORY EXERCISES.—*a.* A method of conducting the preparatory exercises is given in paragraph 76.

b. Each assistant instructor is assigned a target and conducts the preparatory training and firing of all groups on his target.

c. In preparatory training, coach and pupil should change places frequently.

d. Forty-five minutes at each type of target should be sufficient to train each soldier in the preparatory exercises.

e. A detail of one noncommissioned officer and four or six men should be provided to operate each type of target.

SECTION V

FIELD TARGET FIRING

■ 114. PREPARATION.—The instructor should secure necessary equipment, inspect ranges, and detail and train necessary assistants, including demonstration units, prior· to the first period of instruction. Instructors should use their initiative in arranging additional exercises in the application of the principles herein contained. It should be explained to trainees how the exercises used illustrate the principles in the technique of marksmanship in field target firing. Good work as well as errors in the conduct of the exercises should be called to the attention of all trainees.

INDEX

INDEX

INDEX

O

Milton Keynes UK
Ingram Content Group UK Ltd.
UKHW041053290923
429627UK00001B/131